Cowshit Strawberries

Written and Illustrated

by

Vera Rockwell Coghill

The Learmonth Press

First Edition
June 2007
Published by
The Learmonth Press
Edinburgh
EH4 1PT
isbn 978-0-9555640-0-0

learmonthpress@btinternet.com

In memory of
Mama and Pop

Elizabeth Hinman Carl & Stephen E Rockwell

Bessie and Stevie

Mama& Pop

C 1909

Prologue

Today I sit here in my top floor window looking out at a line of 'Edinburgh backs'. They are the other side of the square of houses which make up this typical 'almost' New Town part of Edinburgh – just over the Dean bridge as one comes out of the town. Sitting beside me, in my head, in my heart and at the end of my drawing pen is the child whose story this is. We are a long way from the rural Connecticut hamlet in which we were born and where our story began over seventy years ago.

It is a story based on that mixture of memory and imagination most of us employ in an attempt to make and keep a sense of who we are – the reality that informs our being. The internal map written in one's brain, based on personal experience and the need to make real one's thoughts and feelings, is unique. No two people perceive the world in exactly the same way. So to the question, 'Is it true?' the answer must be, 'Yes, mostly'. It is as true as my memory, mixed as it is with my personal map of reality, can allow it to be.

None of it exists today; some of it may never have, except in my child's imagination, but nevertheless for me it is and was real and as I remember it.

The small town, Hawleyville, is still there in Connecticut. You can see the schoolhouse, the railway track and the store, which is now a Post Office only. My mother and father are buried in the cemetery, their headstone sinking somewhat in the hollow of their graves and the tree above grown out of all proportion to memory. The swimming hole is shrunk to a weedy almost stagnant pond and the sandpit in the disused railway cutting is over grown with weeds and, what amounts to, trees. The brook has been diverted and dammed to form a landscaped pond in front of a house built on the cow-lot in front of Pop's house. His house now gentrified and almost too pretty, still stands on the hill behind the thinner line of maple trees

The rural countryside of my childhood in Fairfield County with its green rounded wooded hills, open spaces, dirt roads, cow studded fields and small family farms no longer exists. It has been criss-crossed with large highways making Hartford or the sea an easy drive. My early life was confined by the parameters of poverty and relative distance. Most of it took place within an easy walking distance of our house in an era that is now extinct. In fact it was almost an anachronism then; we were on the cusp. Electricity had come to our small town but not to the road where we lived.

The child that sits here with me – for it is her story – will draw you a map so you may understand where she comes from. A difficulty as I have been writing this account has been to separate the child from the observing adult. I have never quite come to terms with which voice speaks best for the child – hers or mine. Therefore the reader may have to make imaginative jumps as we – adult and child - change tense and voice mid-paragraph.

Introduction

The Hawleyville of today is nothing like the one of my barefoot past; neither does it resemble the original rail road town it was during its own glorious years.

It was a major player in the development of New England's rail travel in the mid 1800's. In 1849 the Housatonic Railroad was completed between Bridgeport Connecticut and Pittsfield Mass. It needed to pass through the area then known as Land's End which was principally farm and woodland. Much of it belonged to the Hawley family. The new line required some of the Hawley land which was requisitioned by the state. In return for this demand Glover Hawley wanted the town named Hawleyville.

By about 1880 several important lines converged in Hawleyville and the quiet hamlet became a major junction. There was a station, a turntable and switching equipment. It became a busy town with a hotel situated near the station. 'The Newtown Bee' in 1883 reported '60 trains per day passing through Hawleyville'. Another report quotes the longtime station agent Jesse James saying in 1900 that '153 trains of all sorts passed through daily'.

It was the railroad that brought my parents to Hawleyville in about 1912 or so. Pop worked the rest of his life on the railroad, latterly for the NYNH&Hartford RR. He was proud to be a member of 'The Brotherhood of Railroad Trainmen'. He worked in the station at first, presumably under Jesse James. When the importance of Hawleyville declined with the gradual demise of railroad travel and the rise of the motorcar and the station no longer in use, he worked on the tracks.

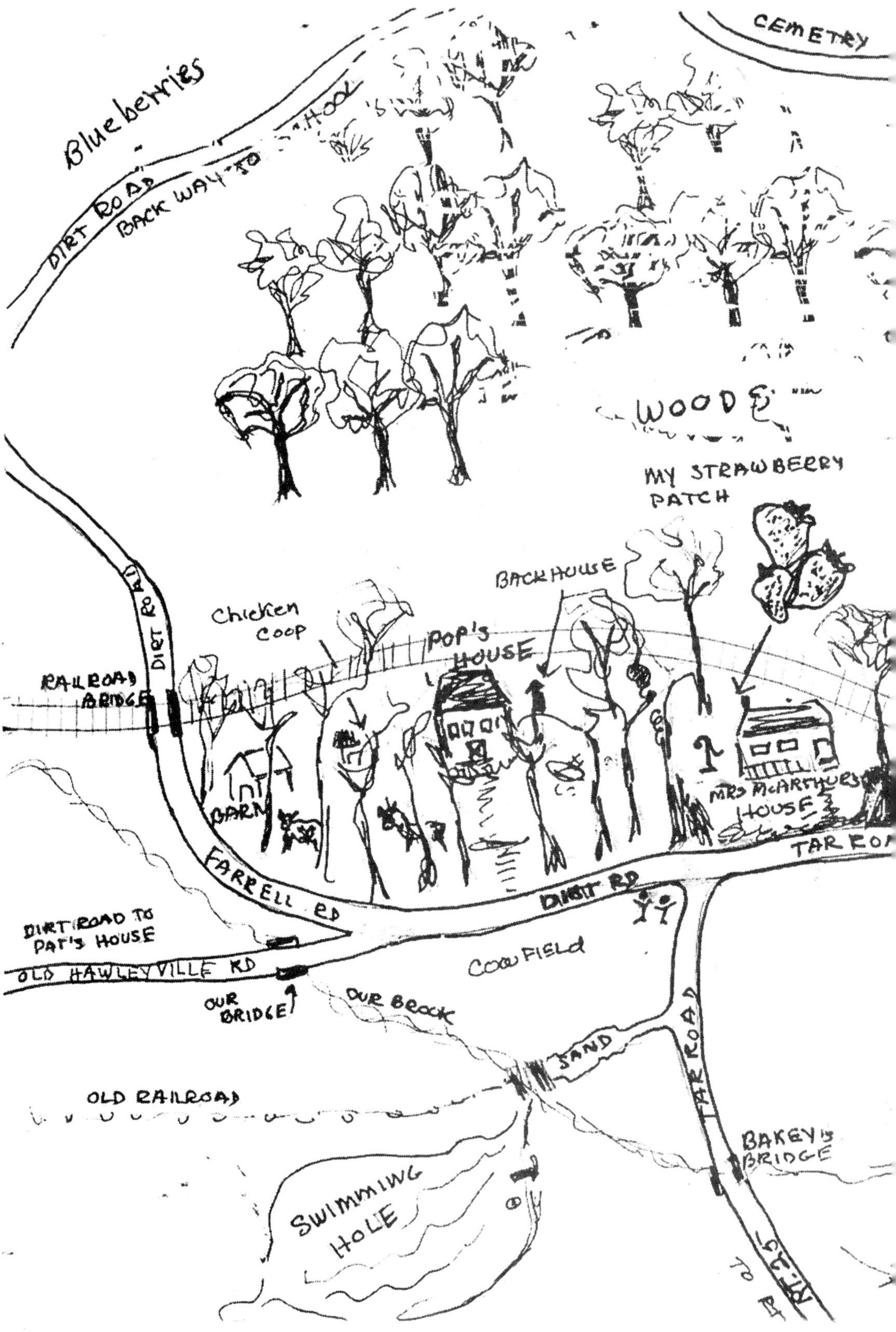
Blueberries
CEMETERY
DIRT ROAD
BACK WAY TO SCHOOL
WOODS
MY STRAWBERRY PATCH
BACKHOUSE
Chicken coop
POP'S HOUSE
RAILROAD BRIDGE
DIRT RD
BARN
MRS McARTHURS HOUSE
TAR ROAD
FARRELL RD
DIRT RD
DIRT ROAD TO PAT'S HOUSE
OLD HAWLEYVILLE RD
COW FIELD
OUR BRIDGE
OUR BROOK
SAND
OLD RAILROAD
TAR ROAD
BAKEY'S BRIDGE
SWIMMING HOLE
RT. 25

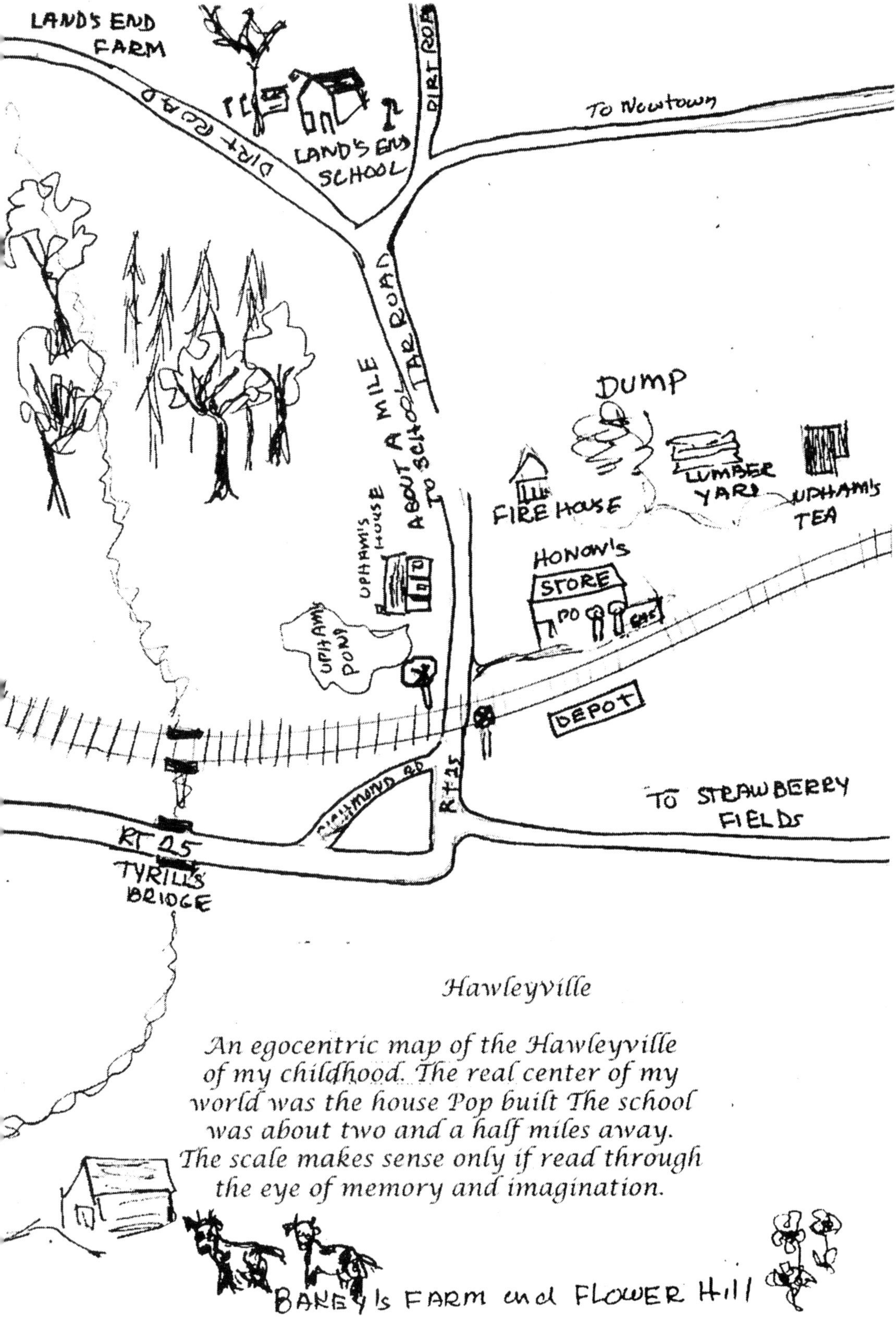

Hawleyville

An egocentric map of the Hawleyville of my childhood. The real center of my world was the house Pop built The school was about two and a half miles away. The scale makes sense only if read through the eye of memory and imagination.

Wild Strawberries

I know where some strawberries grow
As big as teacups, don't you know.
But I'm not telling you.

I've watched them there when they grew
From small white stars, don't you know.
Listen- what I'm telling you.

I'll take the dog down, now they've grown,
He'll bark and bark and he won't moan.
But I'm not taking you.

They are red and sweet and fully ripe
Just ready for a thief to swipe.
So I'm not taking you.

They're mine, all mine. I've watched them grow
As big as saucers, don't you know.
None of them for you.

They are red and sweet and hanging thick
Just waiting there for me to pick.
No, I'm not taking you.

They're mine, all mine. I've watched them grow
As big as plates now, don't you know.
So I'm going down without you.

There, there, there they are, as red as red,
Just bursting from their shady bed.
Mine all mine, don't you know.

I've eaten tons but still they glow
All red as red, don't you know.
But I'm not sharing them with you.

They're mine all mine. The red river flows
All down my hands, bare feet and toes,
Shoulders, face and arms and nose.

Rubbed in my hair and down my chin
Strawberry juice has burned my skin
In summer's secret sin.

Next - comes the fun, now don't you know.
'Cause here is where the cow paths go.
Along the fence in a long, long row

Cow pats baking in the sun
I step in each -one by one.
Green juices bathe my strawberry toes,
As cow perfume gets up my nose.

I know where some strawberries grew.
Next year maybe I'll take you.

Abbreviated Family Tree

Mama and Pop were first cousins.Their common ancestors are Elijah Porter Hinman and Mary L Hobbs who had several children including Elizabeth [Pierce] b 1835 and Williamb b 1840. Pop was desended from Elizabeth and Mama from William

****

Elizabeth Hinman Pierce
mother of
Julia Myrtilla Pierce b1860
married
George Rockwell b1848

William Hinman
father of
Jennie E Hinman b1864
married
Rodney Carl b1860

Grandma & Grandpa Rockwell had four children including twins Stephen [Pop] &Gaylord, Ruby and Alfred

Grandma & Grandpa Carl had five chrildren Leal Elizabeth [Mama], Maude Joyce and Issac

Gaylord & Stephen

Elizabeth & Leal

Elizabeth b1890 m Stephen b1881

They had thirteen children

Chapter One

All The Rockies

All the Rockies in the Dell
They all know but they won't tell.

There they are. Here they come. Quick! Pop'll be mad if we don't get there.

Bare feet pound out of the dooryard, down the stony path, past the woodpile, out onto the dirt road, up the small hill to the railroad bridge.

We made it. There they are, Pop and "Garibaldi" singing at the tops of their voices, one on each side of the handle of the dolly-car pumping themselves around the corner, coming down the straight track until they stop just the other side of the bridge where we wait with the rope already tied on the handle of Pop's battered black lunch box. Send 'er down", he yells and we strain to see the box freefall and then take up the slack of the rope. One of the boys then

jumps up on the side of the bridge to see and slowly lowers the box down. Pop unties it, we pull up the rope and off they go, Pop and his workmate pumping the lever and singing their way to Hawleyville.

We go working on the railway
All the livelong day.
We go working on the rail way
Just to pass the time away-ie-ie-ieeee

Us kids might linger a while, throwing things over the bridge to watch them spin their way to the bottom. Best of all were maple tree seeds but they were long gone. This was high summer and any old bit of paper would do as it slowly spun its way to the bottom. Then we were off.

We might go back, Jimmy and me, to work on our town. It took up a sizeable part of the dooryard. Digging in the hard packed dirt we had an elaborate series of tunnels, roads and buildings which we fought about, cried over when they collapsed in a sudden downpour, then carefully reconstructed until at some time we abandoned them altogether in our attempt to dig to

Australia or China. How many years did we work on that town? How many months, days, hours or minutes did it take until we grew out of that and into something else? How many spoons did we ruin, bent over double by the hard earth? How many prisoners of war did we take out through our yard? Was "Garibaldi" really the Gaibaldi in one of Pop's books or was he, perhaps, a prisoner of war? In any case, it was he who sang:

All the Rockies in the dell
They all know but they won't tell.

Won't tell what? Won't tell about him being a prisoner of war? Besides we don't live in a dell; we live on a hill.

Our house sat on top of the hill on a ragged long triangle of land. On the back side there was a fence to keep us from the railroad bank, in front was the road that curved down into a dip and back up again with another road off it just to the left of the front of the house. The other side of the triangle was a stonewall which marked our property from the lots beside Mrs.MacArthur's and us. The hill rose in an ellipse. At the highest point stood the house built into the bank of the hill with a steep, little used front path down to the road. All along the roadside were maple trees.

Our house was as important a character in this story as the people and I'll tell you about it soon. This is essentially my story,Vera MayBelle Rockwell (1933),the youngest of the Hawleyville tribe who all lived there but never all at the same time. My nearest companions were the two brothers immediately older than me, Halsie and Jimmy.

Da'ya know you're your own third cousin?

No I ain't. I'm your sister. And I'm an aunt. I was an aunt as soon as I was born.

Yah but... you are my third cousin and so you are your own third cousin. So there.

Jimmy and I might then get into one of those 'you are, I'm not, you are' arguments that Jimmy, who was two and a half years older than me, was sure to win. He might appeal to an older brother, Halsie or Jiggy to back him up.

Ain't she? Aint't she her own third cousin?

Yah she is. Pop and Ma are second cousins and so that makes us third cousins.

Ya..ya.ya.yaya

Told ya so. AND we're related to Norman Rockwell and we came over on the Mayflower!

Such were the taunts and boasts that introduced me to the idea of relations and ancestry, to that part of my history that already existed before I did. One myth can be killed immediately. There were no Rockwells on the Mayflower. But several are known to have settled in New England in the mid 1600's. Most particularly, a John Rockwell in Stamford Connecticut in 1641 to whom our lineage can be traced. It transpires that his son Jonathan (1665) was the common ancestor of the Hawleyville Rockwells and of Norman P Rockwell the painter and illustrator. Our grandfather, George, was the great, great, great grandson of Jonathan, and, Norman Rockwell was the great, great, great, great, great grandson of this same Jonathan. I cannot calculate the relationship but it does exist no matter how tenuous. When I was small Norman Rockwell was already famous for his covers of 'The Saturday Evening Post' and somebody told me that Grandma Rockwell got

Christmas cards from him but I never saw any so do not know the truth of this.

Pop and Mama were second cousins because their mothers were first cousins. I am my own third cousin! The childhood refrain rings true.

I never knew my Grandpa Rockwell he died long before I was born but I knew about him. He was a cabinetmaker and wheelwright. He made all of the furniture in their house.
My Grandma Rockwell I did know. She was a very small, bird like, old lady with a withered and twisted face having had Bell's palsy. Her eyelid drooped; constant tears ran down her cheek that she wiped with a small white handkerchief. She kept this in a hole in the cane my father especially carved for her; it was a sort of bird head with the hole for the hankie a part of the design. It was a beautiful stick made from some kind of quite pale wood. Although she was always kind to me and called me 'Little Vera', as a small child I was somewhat frightened of her because of her twisted face. She was also very deaf and and so talking to her became a series of shouts, nods and grunts. I used to think Pop was bawling

her out like he did us if we were naughty. She lived on her own near Danbury Ct. in what we called 'the mountain house' because it sat against a hill that rose straight up behind it.

Her house was full of delightful things especially those in a glass fronted cabinet. She sometimes took some out for me to see. There was a little chick eggcup I particularally liked. It was also full of books and piles of magazines including, of course, "The Saturday Evenings Post" featuring Norman Rockwell covers. It was always cool and quiet there except when Pop was ranting or when she listened to the radio leaning her head against it to 'hear' the vibrations. She lived there alone until she was 96.

My Grandma and Grandfather Carl, Mama's mother and father, had a farm near Afton New York. He also died before I was born and the only things I know about him are that he was strict, a great churchman and his children were not allowed to play on Sundays, that he had a beautiful tenor voice and that he formed his family, who also had 'true' voices into a choir, and that he suffered from 'sick headaches' when he became a bad tempered tyrant. Grandma Carl I did see a few times; she looked a lot like Mama but sat in her rocking chair in the farmhouse kitchen I remember vividly seeing her lather her face and shave every morning. I was fastinated by this ritual and stood and stared but she didn't seem to mind. She, like the rest of the woman in our family, was a skilled needlewoman and like my Mama loved to sing.

Pop worked most of his life for the NewYork,New Haven &Hartford Rail Road. But in his young days he had other ambitions. All his life he read, wrote poetry, argued politics and had the reputation of being somewhat of a 'hellraiser'. Although he graduated from High School at 15 and received no further education, Pop became a schoolteacher for a time in Bainbridge NY, near to where Mama lived and I imagine that is where they got to know each other as he was born in Connecticut and she in New York. He, so the story goes, was sweet on a girl called Viola and made her pregnant but her parents would not let them marry. He then chose Elizabeth, they married around about 1909. They lived at first in Danbury but soon after their first child Rodney Carl, known always as Carl, was born they settled in Hawleyville where they continued to live throughout their life. There was a baby more or less every two years. Carl, the eldest, was nearly 25 years older than me, the youngest.

We were the Rockwells – known collectively and individually as "Rockies" .Rodney Carl (1910), Viola Elizabeth (1912), George Stephen (1914), Mary Virginia (1916), Martha Lois (1917), John Grenville (1919), Benjamin Pierce (1920), Jesse David (1922), Corona Vivien (1923), William Edmond (1925), Halcyon Ernest (1927), James Theodore (1931), Vera Maybelle (1933).

, All the Rockies 1936 at the 4th July picnic clockwise from left:

Carl, Libby, George Mary, Martha , Johnny, Benny, Jiggy, Tonie, Billy, Halsie, Jimmy, Me

Chapter Two

The House That Pop Built

Family stories became myths, myths became truths; they are all fables or fabrications. Each person embroiders or enhances the tale as the spirit moves. As the last Rockie I inherited many such half-remembered 'truths' that no doubt were not entirely made up.

'Once when he was a little kid, about two, Pop burned down his house. He was playing with matches and it burned down to the ground. Grandma didn't like him as much as she did his twin, ya' know?'

This tale was often repeated as me and Jimmy were building illicit fires, or burning holes into newspaper by using a magnifying glass. Sometimes we burned black spots into Mama's petunias that grew near the path up beside the backhouse. But I'm getting ahead myself. I'm not even born yet!

'Pop built our house. He got it out of the Sears and Roebuck catalogue'
'He couldn't 'ave; it's too big for the post office, 'n I've never seen a house in the catalogue.'
'He did. Jiggy told me so, 'n he had nine children living in a tent until it was built.'

Halsie even showed me the barn on somebody's lot where the tent was supposed to be stored. When I asked him if he ever saw it,

'nah it's all in holes now!'

There are various versions of the family's nomadic past. Carl was born in Danbury but Libby, about 18 months younger was born in Hawleyville. They had their picture taken with Mama.

In 1997 when I began this story, or history, I wrote to the five other surviving kids asking for information about our past (incidentally, we all grew to adulthood and, apart from Libby who died at 36 from cancer and Billy who died of a cerebral accident at 42, it was old age, diabetes and heart disease that thinned us out). Tonie's children were afraid I'd 'steal all the stories' as she too was writing her memories and Martha , or Pat as we called her, wrote a letter saying she was also writing our history but gave me these 'facts'

> 'Mom and Pop lived in Danbury when they were first married – I believe on Division Street. When they moved to Hawleyville they lived in what they referred to as "the old store" meaning on the corner where the Van Valkenbergs lived.From there they went to Mrs. MacArthur's house. We were living there when Pop got the property to build the house. In 1923 we moved up on the hill into the Allen house. In 1924 we moved to the upstairs part of Monica Miller's house. In March 1925 we moved in The House.'

She scotched the idea that they had lived in a tent; she was probably right but it was one of the myths I totally believed and used as an example when quoting Jimmy's grown up assertion that 'Pop was the original hippy'.

The ever-expanding family must have presented ever-increasing problems of accommodation in these rented places. Nobody seems to know how long they stayed 'put' after each move but I have counted five moves in about 15 years. The last three moves happened within three years with as many as eight and then nine children under 15 years old and a new baby born during the final move. This child, Billy, was the only one to have been born in hospital; Mama went into hospital from one house and came home with the new baby to the house that Pop built. It seems Pop had a falling out with Mrs. Miller and moved out in a huff and installed the family into his house whilst it was still just a shell. That made ten kids and two adults living under one roof. A complete roof was about all it had at first. The year was 1925. It was never entirely finished until after Pop's death in 1947.

It must have been pandemonium when they first moved with all those little kids charging about. The upstairs was only half floored. The story went that Pop put up paper walls to partition off the downstairs rooms and the kids used to run and jump through these walls causing him to shout and swear and put on another layer of paper. By the time I appeared, the walls were made of plaster board and this was just another family story but I believe it to be true.

Pop had ordered the house from Sears. They were noted for their pre-cut, pre-planned houses that could be ordered from their special catalogue of Homes and shipped by rail to the nearest depot. Ours came into Hawleyville. It was possible to 'customize' the house to your own specification by 'shopping' in the catalogue, a bit like shopping on the internet today.

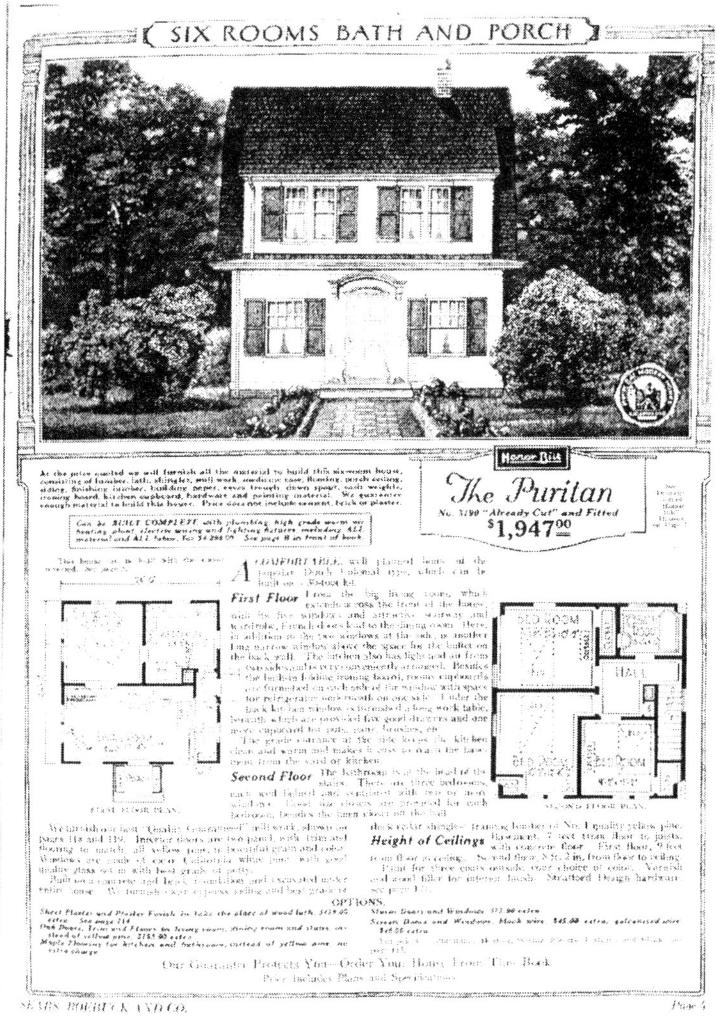

The Sears Illustration of The Puritan[1]

1 Downloaded from internet.©Sears Roebuck

I can imagine Mama and Pop pouring over the pages with the help of half a dozen kids. I found the 1920-1926 Sears Home 'book' on the internet and cannot identify exactly which house they chose but the one named 'The Puritan' seems most like the plan and look of Pop's house. It differs in that I know a porch was planned to run all the way across the front and I think the facia of the front was also straight across unlike the one illustrated. It was two storeys and the room layout and stairs similar except that it was reversed. Interestingly this is a possibility stated in the plans.

Apparently Pop had a carpenter called Cliff Maynard helping the family build it. First they had to dig the cellar. They decided to build the house on the top of a rather steep hill and so the cellar had earth walls at the back and part way along each side. Then the foundations were of stone. Built like a stonewall made by a rather inept farmer, they were open to the elements winter and summer. I think he must have been frantic to get the house finished. However the house itself was weather proof and well constructed and still stands.

I remember it so well. It stood cut into the hill with the stone foundations making it seem taller because there was nothing to stop the eye except the boarded up opening where the front door ought to have been. Good thing it was boarded up because if you had stepped out you would have fallen several feet onto the ground and then rolled down the bank. As long as Pop lived, it never got the porch where Mama should have sat to rock her babies as she sang to them about the trees, the brook and the pussy-willows blowing low into the water. The house was to stay perched up upon the stones loosely piled into foundations until the Rockies no longer lived there. Mama sat in the kitchen or on the big rock in the cool of the side of the house, or sometimes with me on the doorstep outside the kitchen as I drank my cocoa and milk and she her tea. She might be at her sewing machine in the corner of the kitchen, or beside the pot-bellied stove in the other room. Pop built the house; Mama made the home.

Chapter Three
The Black House With Holes

Our house was almost as eccentric as was Pop.

As well as the missing porch and front door, it was covered with black tarpaper instead of cladding. Just as a temporary, preparatory measure until it could be clapboarded. It never got the outer cover in our time. In places the black tarpaper had been torn away to expose the weathered boards underneath. Some parts had been patched with gray or green tarpaper. It was a patchwork house.

By the time I was old enough to be running about the dooryard, two of my older sisters had left home and started families of their own. Libby already had two girls before I was born, Betty and Barbara. Mary had two soon afterwards, Susan and Blanche. It was one of Mary's girls, Susan, whose

Standing at the kitchen door

poetic description most nearly fits the house. Susan was about three and Blanche a little younger when Mary came to stay for a short time while she looked for a new home. It was fun for me to have girls to play with. There were three boys immediately older than me and my youngest sister, Tonie, was already ten when I was born. I was about five when they came to stay and not used to company for my doll play. It was fun but in a few weeks Mary had found another place to stay. When Susan was told she was going to live in a new house she screamed, "I don't want to. I want to live in an old house. I want to live in a black house with holes in it with Grandma."

Not only was it a patchwork house it was also a back-to-front house, since the only entrance was through the kitchen at the side rear.

A rough plan of the downstairs as I remember it

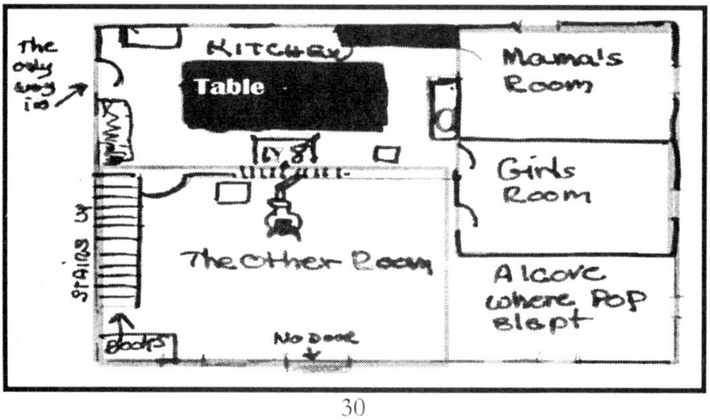

The kitchen was the true center, the hub of life. Mama sits here. I watch her. A fly buzzes its way around and lands on her arm. She hardly moves and doesn't notice as it makes its way down her arm and slowly creeps onto the oilcloth to land first in the sugar and then in the butter before it zizzes upward to stick with its friends on the spotted coil of fly paper hanging from the ceiling. Sometimes it's my job to pull out the new flypaper from its cartridge case and hold it up, all sticky and new smelling, ready for the next batch of invaders. I quite like flies. I know I like butter and sugar as I lick my finger and put it first in the soft butter and then into the sugar bowl and run out the door before I get caught on flypaper.

Mama peeling apples

Behind the kitchen door were coat hooks which hung with an accumulation of out door clothes in various states of repair, age and size. In a pile, which grew year on year on the floor behind the door, was an assortment of footwear. If you were desperate to make a trip up the hill to the backhouse and it was frosty or snowy you could usually find something to put your feet into. Size didn't much matter as long as you could keep them on long enough for the trip there and back.

Along the kitchen back wall were two windows just the right height to climb in and out and this was a summer alternative to the back door. In winter Jack Frost decorated them in the most beautiful lace patterns. Mama's sewing machine was behind the door next to the first window. It was a treadle and it hummed away as her feet went faster and faster. I used to sit between her feet on the treadle to get a free ride as she worked away. I think I was helping her. Pop's chair was on this side between the two windows and in front of a large mirror. In the other corner on that back wall was a huge cupboard where dishes and other stuff were kept. That was where the mixing bowl for bread lived and also the brown jar that kept the yeast in the dark so it wouldn't 'go off'. For a long time I thought this meant it might explode like a firecracker, but once it did 'go off' and it was just a stodgy yellowish green sticky mess.

On the next wall was the door into Mama's room. Next to that was the sink and draining board. No water pipes came up to give us water instead it was brought by the pail full from the brook or Mrs. MacArthur's pump. There was a small flyspecked mirror where the older boys shaved and Pop trimmed his moustache and shaved around it.

Hanging from a nail was the leather strop that Pop used to sharpen his 'cut-throat'. All round about the sink were piled dishes either dirty or clean or both except on the odd times when somebody had had a good clear up and put everything in the cupboard. When it wasn't blocked, there was a drain hole to let the water away. When it was blocked, you had to throw the water out the back door. The drainpipe was connected underground to a cesspool that had a habit of getting clogged and then had to be dug up and "seen to".

Further along from the sink was a door into another bedroom. I think this was called the "girls room" but I remember boys sleeping there. Against the wall next to this door stood the wooden icebox. It sat up on little legs with a basin underneath to catch the dripping water. Alongside it was a small stool to put the pail of drinking water with its enamel dipper. We all drank straight from the dipper. It was white with a blue edge and a big black chip surrounded by rust in the very middle of it. Pop said it will spring a leak and we need a new one but it never did and we didn't ever get a new one.

Next to the ice box the big black range sat out from the wall. Its stove pipe, hung with cobwebs, disappeared into the wall behind leaving the stove standing on its own. Behind, just beside the wood piled up ready and the coal pail when we had some, was room for a box with a pillow on it; just right to curl up and read. Or better still curl next to somebody and be read to.

The range had a firebox with lids that lifted off with a special removable handle. There was a hot water tank at the other side. Above were small cupboards to keep things in. Mama's special graham crackers lived in the first one; crackers to have with soup in the other. There was an oven to one side between the firebox and the hot water tank. Under the fire was the ash pan. All along the front was a shiny solid rail where anybody could lean and warm their butt. You could tell when the fire was hot enough to cook by spitting on the lid. The hotter the fire the faster the spitball sizzled and danced. Here the flat irons were put to heat in a small row. The handles were separate and you operated a little spring release to put them on and off. You tested their heat with spit too but this time you wet your finger with it in just the same way you did if you fancied butter and sugar. If it made a little 'zist', they were hot enough to use. To make toast you took off the lid and held the bread over the open fire on a long fork. I loved toast. This stove played an important role in my life.

Beside the kitchen stove was the door into the "other room". Then all along the next wall were windows that looked over the dooryard. Between the windows stood a dresser with shelves and next to that an oil stove that we used in the summer. The kitchen was quite a big room with linoleum over the wooden floorboards. I can see Mama, with a far away look in her eye, sweeping it with a broom worn into a triangle.

Right in the middle of the kitchen and taking up most of the space was the table. Some of my earliest memories are of the underneath. Jimmy and I played there a lot and the best game was to play at lions and tigers

Pop asleep at the table

snapping and growling at everybody's feet including Pop's. He was safely protected from view by the huge board of the top. The table was unusual in that it had lots of legs. In the center was a pedestal, which splayed out into four magnificent lion's claw legs. As well as this there were four straight legs at each corner of the rectangular top. It was much too big to be removed from the kitchen and when I wanted to know how it got in I was shut up with, "Pop built it here, of course". There was almost room enough round it for the whole family to sit together at Thanksgiving or Christmas when most everybody tried to be home. But before the older girls left home, before I was born, they didn't always have a place to sit. They had to take second shift and wait for the boys who were working to have their supper. There were not enough chairs to go around and benches were made from boards placed across the seats of two chairs for little ones to sit on. We each had our own place. In Tonie's memoir (2003) she names all of our places: 'For meals my mother sat on one side next to the big iron stove. On her left sat Vera who was always getting scolded for sitting with her feet in the chair and for sticking her fingers in the butter, then in the sugar and then licking them off. On mother's right sat Hal who wouldn't eat if onions were anywhere near him. Around the corner from Vera sat Carl. Between Carl and Johnny was Jimmy, around the corner and next sat Benny. Next in the middle opposite my mother, was my father. Next to him sat Jiggy. I sat around the corner at the next side. On a board over two chairs and next to me was Billy. Then George sat next to Hal and that completed the circle around the table.'

As well as being extra long the table was extra wide too. Once when Billy was playing with an old portable sewing machine set up on the table across from Pop's chair he sewed through his finger and fainted. Pop jumped right over the table to pick him up. Pop was the only one to have a chair with arms. It sat in the middle of the long side opposite the stove between the windows. Years later when he finally lived there alone he still occupied the same place.

I can remember sitting on Pop's lap about eye level with the table. One of the kids has come home to visit. I think it may have been Mary but I truly don't remember. It is already dark outside and in the corners of the room. The lamps are alight. The big one, in the middle of the table, glows greenly casting its circle of light onto the table and bringing alive the shadow family that mimics the movements of my own real family only bigger. Both move in time with each other but the less solid shadows move and bend and flee into the dark corners while the real faces are brightly lit in the flickering light. It seems to be a celebration. It definitely concerns me. I think it could have been my second birthday. Certainly I am very small. It is warm with happiness. I look across the great expanse of table. The other side is as far away as across the room is to me now. The faces are large and laughing and seem to glow, especially the eyes. A gray toy dog with a red coat is produced from darkness and caused to stand just out of the circle of light on the opposite side of the table from me. A pathway is cleared. It must have been a clockwork toy. Anyway the dog walks across the table to me getting bigger and bigger and bigger - it shines in the light and I reach out. It is still too far away but encouraged by my laughing and shouting it comes nearer and nearer. Happiness burns into my eyes this never to be forgotten scene and burns my hands with gleeful power when I actually catch the dog and send it walking away back again across the table to other waiting hands. That kitchen table was the stage for many other dramas, which made up my childhood.

I catch the dog

Outside the kitchen was the dooryard. This was hard packed earth where the chickens came to scratch and we played much of the time. Along the hillside was a stone wall which meandered along and down the gentle hill towards the barn and chicken-coop. The dooryard was more or less level and the hill rose behind the wall. At the front the yard ended abruptly in about a five-foot drop where there was another more solid wall that formed the entrance to the cellar. There were stone steps from one level to the next about six feet away from the house. We didn't have cellar doors to slide down. This was the way into the cellar.

Dare you
Double dare
Double, double dare you.

NO

Go on scaredy cat. Go in and shut the door.

Noooooo let me oooooout.

The cellar was dark and smelled of damp earth, mice and must. If you dared to go in and shut the door you could always see pinpoints of daylight along two sides once your eyes got used to the dark and nothing but blackness the further back you looked. Because it was dug out of the ground with loosely piled foundation stones in the front; the further back you went the nearer to extinction you came. The cellar door was big and heavy, made of rough boards with rusty hinges and a latch that didn't meet the hook into which it should fasten. Inside, the cellar was always cold even on the hottest day. In the winter snow sifted through the chinks in the stones and made white drifts to shine in the darkness along the front wall. "Good insulation", Pop said.

The only time I went there voluntarily was for the secret drinking of home made root beer which lived in dusty boxes away near the back or stood in lines on the dirt floor. Even then we would only dare this if the cellar door was left open and a shaft of light connected the interior with known life outside. We liked to work the patent capping machine that put gold eyes on the brown or green bottles of soda. I wonder if Pop didn't have something stronger than root beer stored there sometimes, he was partial to cider and elderberry wine, but it was root beer that was our goal.

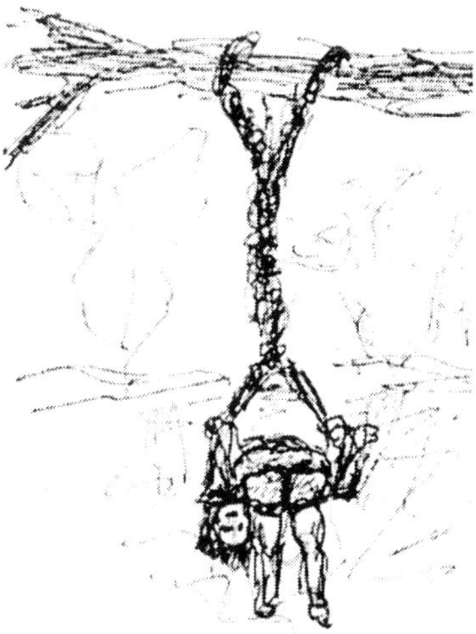

Outside in the light again I might run down and have a swing. The swing was a rope tied to the branch of the biggest tree in the front of the house. The seat a board with two triangles cut in the ends to fit onto the rope. When swinging and singing palled there was always twisting up in the rope until the space for my knees was so tight it cut before I "let 'er rip" and spun to the end, jerked around and spun again until giddiness forced me to dig my bare toes into the dirt, jump off and go someplace else.

Across the front of the house, next to the stone foundations was a shallow bank leading down to a levelled area that was to be the lawn. This was where my swing tree stood with a few other trees. Not much else happened in the front yard. It was a good growing place for poison ivy. There wasn't enough grass to stake the cows on, or enough dirt to dig in, nor was it big enough for ball playing and much too bumpy and stony for rolling across. Further down in front, past the levelled area was a sheer drop down to the road, fringed I think, by a stone wall and swallowed by undergrowth. In the center was a steep path down to the road. This was just trampled earth but had a few stone steps for the steepest part. It was the quick way down to the brook; most of our water for clothes washing was carried up this path.

At the end of the front yard, on the opposite side from my swing tree, was THE WELL. The well lay on forbidden territory and I never dared risk it. Not often anyway. The topmost opening was freely accessible, a large crater but shallow like the beginning of a pond. When I say shallow, it was deep enough for a grown-up to stand upright and just see over the top. The excavated earth piled up around the rim defined the parameter. Standing on the bank above, it looked like an enormous spot made in the dust by an oversized raindrop, except that it was as dry as dry. In the center was a shaft. It went down exactly one ladder length. I know because the ladder was still in it only just visible under the boards placed over the top and weighted down with boulders to keep out the kids. Most of the other kids had been down it but not me. That well was never to get a pump like Mrs. MacArthur's. Sometimes, after a lot of rain or in the spring, there would be a frenzy of activity when water was discovered. My brothers would hopefully measure the depth by dropping down a stick on a rope but there was never enough to convince anyone of the wisdom of starting the digging again although it was talked about a lot. It was always to remain a dry well; Rockwell's well with no water. Why dig a well halfway up a hill?

Up the bank beside the well was the "other side" of the house, so called because it was opposite the dooryard. "Where are the other kids? On the other side fixing cars". On this side the rise of the hill gradually took one up to the driveway, or lane, which came in from the road. There were always two or three cars here in various states of disrepair. Somebody always had an engine out or some other major overhaul in progress. Jimmy and I went for long trips in those cars; him driving and me hanging on the running board or in the rumble seat, sometime me driving and him shouting instructions. Occasionally I really did ride the running board up the driveway and home from the store. Up at the corner of the house on this side under the roof was where the telephone wires were attached. The telephone was our only concession to technology. We never did get wired up to the electricity supply.

At the back of the house, close to the wall was a narrow path between the house and the hill. There was a big flat low stone here where Ma and Pop sometimes sat in the cool, side by side and talked. The path went past Mama's bedroom windows, past the kitchen windows to the door. Along this path the tarpaper was torn and holey, helped no doubt by young vandal hands. This was the way into the black house with holes.

Inside again. The kitchen has four doorways, one in from outside, one into Mama's room, the third to the "girls' room" and a fourth into the "other room". This "other" room ran all across the front of the house; it was really two rooms with an archway. Sometimes this arch was closed off with curtains sometimes not. Inside it was a sleeping area with two beds. In the center of the front room, well out from the wall and connected to the chimney by an 'L' stovepipe, was a 'pot-bellied' stove. You'll hear more about that later.

If you were standing in the doorway from the kitchen, the arch was on the left and over to the right was a cubicle space completely filled with books stacked in, under and around a large table. The door and passageway to the stairs was there on the far right but unseen if you came in from the kitchen door as the stairs led up toward the back of the house and were closed in.

The stairs themselves were steep and always dark. The steps bore an accumulation of old shoes, books, magazines and other momentarily or permanently discarded paraphernalia.

Three-quarters of the way up was a landing and a right-angled turn. Here was a jumble of old sports shoes, shoulder pads, baseball gloves and other musty things. After the turn the last steps brought you into the up-stairs, or more accurately, the attic. This part of the house had never been finished. It was one large room like a barn in which the undersides of the rafters and roof were clearly visible, as was the daylight under the eves. Just under half of the room was floored. The bare boards were smooth against bare feet because they had been so little used. The room was like a dormitory in a school with a whole line of iron beds. It extended the length of the house.

I think there may have been six or seven beds; they varied in size and shape but each had a dirty ticking mattress, some had feather beds, one or two striped dirty white and black specked pillows. The other part of the room that was nearest the stairs was 'floored' only by the ceiling of the rooms below. These ceilings were made from the sides of tea chests nailed underneath the beams. There was a narrow 'cat-walk', I think it was a door laid flat, about three feet wide from the top of the stairs to the floored area. Balanced on the exposed beams were various trunks, boxes, bits or furniture and other saved items. Over in one corner, under the eves on the floored area, sat an old, no longer used kitchen range.

It was certainly not the first time I had been up that stairway. It was familiar in its dark secret-ness. My practiced hands pulled me up, step by step, on all fours nearer and nearer to the light at the top. I have no memory at all of teetering on the edge, or whether I was upright or on my hands and knees when it happened. The memory is of plunging face first and down forever through the jagged edge of the sound of tearing splinters, and of the force of the wind smacking my face as down I plummeted, to land in a tea chest full of pieces that Mama saved for patchwork and then to slip into unknowingness. My next consciousness is of being on the kitchen table with Mama working over me. I am outside my body, up near the ceiling looking down at myself lying there, partly naked where Mama has taken off my clothes. She picks up my arms and legs each in turn and bends them. "She's not dead"', says Mama. In a sensation of white light and movement, I gasp and then am lying looking up at her face as she reaches to hold me. I scream and scream and scream. I have plunged into consciousness of life and of being Rinkie. It happened when I was less then two years old.

She's not dead

Chapter Four

Oven Baked

Birth descriptions are a part of the folklore families manufacture. I was born on October 24 1933 at home in Hawleyville Connecticut USA in the room off the kitchen, Mama's room. It was the only room that had only one door. All of the other rooms were interconnected so that one could, and I frequently did, run round and round, in and out, passing the same spot again and again like a figure in a clockwork tableau. But Mama's room was isolated from the rest.

Of course I cannot remember my own birth in the way I remember falling through the ceiling. My conception of this event is a kaleidoscope of impressions derived from received family lore, manufactured in my imagination, remembered from my unconscious or embodied in that usually untapped primal reservoir of feeling unique to each of us. With the fall through the ceiling came a small death and then the birth of consciousness. My actual birth was no less dramatic, starting as it did with unwillingness to breathe, another small death. I might never have lived if Pop and the "good woman", George's mother-in-law Mabel, who assisted the doctor, had not been as obstinate as me. They worked over my blue form long after many would have given up hope. Slowly life was blown from my father's mouth into my unexpanded lungs. At last, with a small cry, red replaced blue. Then I was wrapped and put into the oven to warm through. An autumn child, a night born child, some might say half-baked.

I never tired of hearing the story of being wrapped and put in the oven. When Mama and I made bread I used to think about being a baby inside the oven beside the tins of bread. Maybe I would get too hot. Or I might cry out like the Gingerbread Boy "Let me out. Let me out". Maybe it didn't happen like that at all maybe the sun it was who heated me through as it did years later to another batch of bread. Maybe, maybe, maybe.

I was born in the early hours; Tonie says they watched through holes in the ceiling from the upstairs because they knew something was happening. As soon as they dared she and all the rest of the little kids came down and stood on the stairs to receive the good news. "It's a girl". Just what was wanted - a girl to break the pattern of boys! There had been three boys in the six years before. Pat, being fifteen at the time, gives her version.' I remember when you were born. It was a very cold day and you turned blue and they wrapped you in a blanket and put you in the open oven to warm you up.I gave you your first soap and water bath when you were three days old. You had been cleaned with oil at birth. I had learned in a nursing club how to do it. I placed a pan of warm water on one chair by the stove and another chair in front of the oven for me to sit on. I had you on a pillow on my lap. And I washed you and dressed you. I stayed home from school a few days to take care of you and Mom'. With my advent the total became what it remained until the death of Libby about twelve years later - five girls and eight boys. A full baker's dozen.

All the Rockies in the dell

They all know but they won't tell.

Chapter Five
Rinkie Turie Jane

"Rinkie, Rinkie", comes the call over the dusk. "Rinkie. Rinkie" sounds through the morning sunshine as I sit watching spiders sitting in the middle of their webs waiting. Rinkie, for that was my baby name, was the thread which trailed behind in my wanderings, anchored me to Mama and guided me safely back to the center of my being. Mama gave me it in my earliest days before a proper name was thought of. I knew no other until I went to school. My birth was not registered until a year and a day after the actual event. I don't think I had to wait that long for a name to be decided upon. It was Pop who had the last say about names and Halcyon and Corona have little to thank him for. (I always thought Corona, or Tonie as I called her, had been named after Pop's typewriter, a Smith-Corona. Perhaps he thought "Peace at last" when he named Halsie.) Eventually, Vera MayBelle was decided upon after my Aunt Vera and my brother George's wife's mother Mabel who was the 'good woman' who attended my birth. I think it was decided by a committee of kids and apparently they asked Mabel how to spell it and she said, 'Just like it sounds' so I became Vera MayBelle. Rinkie was Mama's name for me, which she bestowed with the refrain, Rinkie Turie Jane.

"Rinkie is the baby of the family". How often was I to hear that and repeat it over the years. Libby had two children by the time I was born, Betty and Barbara. Barbara came about two weeks ahead of me; the letters passed in the mail, Mama said. Libby always called me "Baby". Toni was just ten years older than me. She toted me about from a very young age. She remembers taking me to the swimming hole when I was only nine months old. I don't remember going. Toni still holds the memory dear as a measure of the great trust Mama put in her. Certainly my baby days were shared with the rest of the kids and I cannot separate early memories from later ones except in a few instances. Carl could always stop me in my tracks by saying, "I used to change your diapers", if I got too big for my boots.

When I was very little, a dog bit Pat. She couldn't believe that I could remember this. I guess I must have been about eighteen months. There is only just the word "dog" attached to this memory. The rest is visual. What I see is a dark figure outlined against the light. I am way down looking up at it. There is a very big arm shape, pale and in stark, sharp contrast with the rather fuzzy body shape. On this arm is a glowing white patch with an irregular smear, which runs out into the white. It is Indian red and yellow, a stain of color that pulsates and moves. I watch as the white patch is removed and the arm is now the only thing left in the room with me. On it I see a glowing red hole. It seems to pulsate in time to my own heartbeat that I hear for the first time. There are no words or other sounds except for the one word "dog" and that seems to echo from someplace else and is not a part of the tableau. But, in that instant, I know I am not always the center of attention. I am 'me' looking out at the world.

But now I am the main attraction. I am there in the warm lamp light, away down low near people's feet. All eyes are upon me as I sit on

my potty. The circle of faces nod and tilt at me like birds on a fence. I play to the audience with squeals and claps and feet drumming up and down until at last I grunt and out it comes! I stand up and look into the pot. There it is big and shiny, an elegant turd. Mama is very happy with me and I am allowed to pass it around for all to see - my first creative product. Wasn't I clever!

The sharing of this most private function was a part of family life. Pop had built a privy on the hill behind the house. Almost everybody except Mama called it the shithouse. To her it was the backhouse or the outhouse. It was a rather grand one with three holes. There was a big hole, a middle-sized hole and a little hole nearer the floor. Pop had, apparently, built it from an old caboose gleaned from the railroad depot and cut in half. At first Mama or one of the other kids went with me and I sat on the small seat while they sat on a big one. To go up to the toilet alone was one of my first big adventures. To go there at night alone was the absolute terror. I would rather use a pee can.

Inside, the shithouse was dark even on the brightest days. In fact, the brighter the day the darker it was inside. The light pricked into the cracks in the wood to fall in slices of dancing dust across the floor. On a nail was the string to hold the old Montgomery Ward catalogue to wipe your hind end. I could just reach it if I stretched. The smell inside was not as bad as its memory. Flies buzzed away most of the summer. In winter the snow came through the cracks to replace the sunbeams with shafts of white. You didn't linger to plan your catalogue order in the winter. Sometimes Jimmy and I went together and planned what we would buy. He liked looking at the ladies underwear. But it was kids things we wanted and these pages grew worn and thumbed before some unthinking grown up tore them down the middle and sent them onto the heap at the bottom. Mostly there was a quiet peace inside this black retreat where bare feet could kick in tune to an inner song and people kept away.

We were not the only family with a backhouse. It was a favorite trick of our boys to go round and push them over. The story was that somebody pushed one over with Old Man Upham inside. I tried often to push ours over but was not successful even with Jimmy to help. Every few years the pit was filled in as a new one was dug and the privy was moved forward by a width and new grass filled in the brown patch left behind.

The new grass behind the backhouse was lush and long and never eaten by the cows. The sun warmed this little green, green patch. I played there alone with my dolls. I had a rubber dolly. Pink and shiny and smooth like a little piggy it was when new. The best thing was it had a bottle with a rubber teat and it could really drink and pee. It came with diapers and a sun suit but soon it reached the state of most dollies, bare with a scrap of flannelette blanket to wrap it in and ragged bits for diapers.

At first I was content to feed my dolly

water and watch the "pee" drip out the hole at the back. Then I wanted to give it real milk and ran down the hill to Mama in the kitchen.

"No the cows didn't give enough today. No real milk."

So she set to and mixed up a little jar of shoe whitener so I could have pretend real milk. Back up the hill again singing in the sunshine

"Mama's going to buy me a rubber dollieeeee....."

I was happy for a time crooning to my doll as it drank the pretend real milk and then watching as it dripped out as white pee.

"White pee"

No, only real pee would do. Real warm pee was what was needed. So I filled a jar with real pee, carefully poured it into the bottle and attached the teat and fed my dolly alternate feeds of shoe whitener and real pee. She obliged by peeing real warm pee with the right smell. As far as I know nobody ever discovered this. I am sure it would have been stopped if they had. Rinkie had lots of secrets. Mama never knew about the pee soaked rubber doll. Or did she?

At the end of one summer my rubber dolly got left out in the long grass. I couldn't find her and gave up looking. In the spring I came across her all gray and twisted, the color of used bubble-gum, a sodden mass covered with hair-like cracks in a mosaic pattern, sticky where the skin had burst in places and stinking of mould and pee and lost dreams.

Chapter Six

Bread, Milk and Mama

Ours was a large and busy household, not as full by the time I remember it as it once was. I am the baby, of this I am sure and I hold to the position as I hold to my mother's breast, with tenacity. That breast - my Mama.

The story is that I continued, "having titty" until I was five! I expect it was more like two-and-a-half to three. But it is true that I slept with Mama in her bed and Pop slept in one of the beds in the alcove in all the time that I can remember.

Always, always until the day she died Mama came to bed with me. When I was little it was to feed me. I think I can remember that titty. As I got older she came into bed and told me stories and sang songs. When I got still older she came in the night because that is where she slept. I have no conscious memory of being weaned but no doubt it did eventually occur. I do remember clearly a day when Mama disappointed me about milk.

We got most of our milk from the two family cows, Topsy and Peggy. Topsy was red and white and Peggy was a burnt red-brown. A neighbor's cow that was sometimes pastured near ours was called Bessie. Bessie was also Mama's name. That is what Pop called her. This used to puzzle me greatly. Why was Mama named after a cow? The cows were not put out to pasture like the ones from Bakey's farm on the hill. Our cows had a rope halter and were staked out to graze in different spots around the house and barns. They made funny snorts and blows as they chomped at the grass and like so many other children before, and since, I pondered on the wonder of green grass turning to white milk. I couldn't even make pretend white milk turn into pee.

The cows were brought into the barn to be milked night and morning. When he was still at home it was my brother Johnny who usually did the milking. Our song followed him down the hill:

> Johnny went down to milk the cow, parlez-vouz,
> Johnny went down to milk the cow, parlez-vouz,
> He pulled the tail instead of the tit
> And all he got was a bucket of inky, dinky,
> Parlez- voooooooouzz

Sometimes I went along too and had a drink of frothing, foaming hot milk straight from the cow. I squatted down underneath, like a small animal, and it was squirted into my gaping mouth. This method was not quite successful since I could never quite get a mouthful before air forced me to swallow. I did get my face washed.

The best way to drink milk was to find a long hollow grass stem, stick it into the warm, newly milked, brimful pail and suck. The little bluey white bubbles of froth along the rim made a lovely slurpy sound as they were dragged up the straw. The real secret of success was in obtaining the right stem - fairly thick, hollow and not too green but yet not so dry it would collapse. Sucking up new milk was an art. It also required a good pair of cheek muscles. Mine had had plenty of practice.

There were times when one or both cows were "drying off" or waiting to calve and then the two brimful pails of milk might dwindle to just a half pail between them. Was this the reason, as she said, that

Mama refused me, or could it have been that cow's milk was not what I wanted in the first place?

I was about three or four. How can I know because childhood telescopes forward and backward without following the rules of the calendar? Certainly the other children were not there, not even Jimmy. I was home alone with Mama. Outside in the space beside the house, underneath the clothes-line, above the well, alongside the dirt where the boys worked on old cars was a grassy area that grew long and coarse. There was a large wooden box with low sides that us little kids played in. It was a house or a boat or anything else we wanted it to be. That day it was a bed. I had it full of pillows; blue and dirty gray ticking filled with feathers, which were trying to escape. The day was hot with sun and childhood. Indian summer I think because there was a smell in the morning air. I was all-alone in my play and aware of this so maybe Jimmy had just started school. I wanted to be a baby.

So I went into Ma and asked her for a bottle. There was an old black rubber teat still around that I sometimes had on the top of a brown glass Certo bottle which I used for my dolls. She gave me a bottle full of water with the teat in place. I went out again and settled down in my baby box bed swigging down the water. But it wasn't quite right.

Babies drink milk!

So I went in to Mama and she fixed me a bottle of milk. Out I went again, settled down in my bed, took one great swig of milk and nearly choked. It was EVAPORATED MILK. I hated evaporated milk and I would not drink it ever. I went storming back into the house yelling and raging.

"You gave me evaporated milk. I wanted real milk".

Mama smiled and replied.

"There isn't any fresh milk until the cows are milked tonight. Besides, babies drink evaporated milk".

There was no answer to that, as I knew there were pictures of babies on the can. So I went back out to my bed, crying and stamping my feet. I smashed the bottle against a rock, climbed into the box and, like a real baby, took comfort from sucking my thumb. I was first a child playing at being a baby then I was baby me. I discovered what all babies know - that thumb is Mama and that thumb (Mama) and baby are also one. I became a mouth and a thumb and nothing else except sunshine and colors. I was there in that space between time, a space that held me when Mama deserted me for good just a few years later.

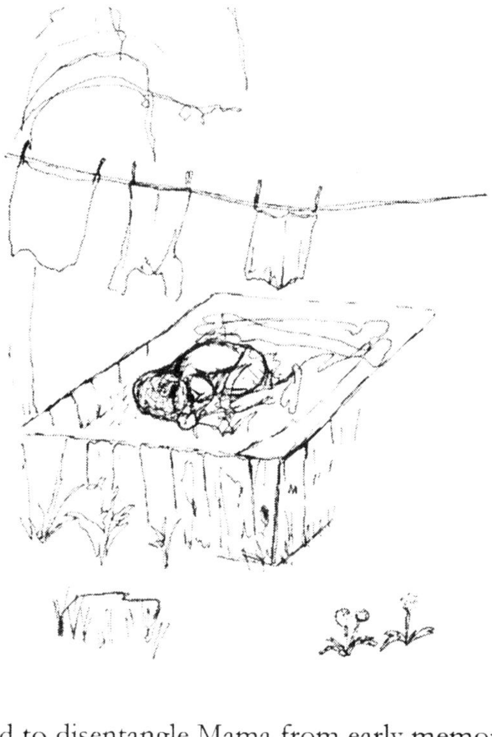

It is hard to disentangle Mama from early memories. She was always there. No matter how far I went into the world the center remained solidly constant. I can picture her now sitting at the far end of the table each morning with a couple of loaves of 'store bought' bread making sandwiches for as many as seven or eight packed lunches. The slices of bread were all laid out, end to end in twos, each with the one that matched it. Then they were generously spread with butter if times were good. During the war we had oleo, a white fat with a small pill of yellow dye which I was allowed to mix but the time I am remembering now is before the war when the older boys were still at home and there were lots of brown paper bags to fill every day and Pop's black lunch box. The sandwiches were made from what ever came to hand. I can remember some hard times later on when my own sandwiches were just oleo with salt and pepper or else salt, pepper, sugar and vinegar sprinkled on some lettuce leaves. I really do not know what went on these pre-war sandwiches but cheese, peanut butter and jelly, and sometimes-leftover meat or chicken I can remember. Occasionally there were "cold cuts" from Honon's store. Store-bought bread was usual for these sandwiches and I can remember the day it went up from ten cents to eleven cents as a black day. I thought we were in real danger of going hungry then! But that was during the war or maybe even after when price ceilings were removed. Pop's lunch was made with home baked bread if there was enough.

The best times with Mama were when the row of brown paper lunch bags was gone and I was left at home with her. An unnatural quiet came over the house. She moved slowly and sat down often when it was just we two. Every morning after the others had left for school I had my second breakfast. It was always cocoa and toast. (I rather liked cocoa made with evaporated milk). In winter or on a baking or washing day when the fire was alight the toast was made by taking off the lid of the range and holding the bread on a fork over the hole where the embers glowed red and black. It always came out perfectly as no toast has before or since. In summer, if the oil stove was used, the toast was burned, or singed, in little knobbles of black that touched the surface but left the inside still soggy. Then the only thing to do with it was to give it a good soaking in cocoa and eat it as sop. Toast was best made with home made bread and it was a bad day if all that was left were the scraps of loaves used for sandwiches.

I don't know how often Mama baked. I think it was about once a week when I was small. Then the stove had to be stoked up, summer or winter, and somebody had to be prodded to go and bring in the wood and some coal if we had any. I took my turn and delighted in the power of being able to carry a whole armful of the short kindling sticks we used to light the range. For bread making the fire had to be nursed along until it was "just right". I knew when it reached "just right" by the click of Mama's tongue and the decided nod of her head. But long before the fire was ready we had the bread making started.

The near end of the table opposite the sandwich making end had to be cleared of dirty dishes, games, newspapers, books and everything else that had accumulated there since the last bread making. For ordinary mealtimes and anything else except a grand "clear up" the stuff could just be pushed to the middle with space enough at the edges to eat or work on. But making bread required space. The oilcloth cover had to be scrubbed at that end - the other end got the same treatment in the mornings when cleared for the lunch preparations. I am not quite sure why that end wouldn't have done for the bread making too. It may have been because it was not near where the flour sack lived or that it was on the darker side of the room. There was always a clutter in the middle of the table of things we needed at mealtimes. The spoon holder which was a jar with table cutlery, the salt box and pepper, an odd jar of jelly or so, peanut butter, bottles of ketchup, pickles, butter dish and sugar bowl were jumbled together and were rarely disturbed by the scrubbing cloth.

Bread making took precedence over most things. We donned our flour sack aprons. Then Mama became a powerhouse of energy. First the enormous mixing bowl, yellow ochre outside and creamy crazed glaze inside with a stained crack on the rim, arrived down from its place on top of the kitchen cupboard. Milk was scalded in a small pan and set aside to cool and await the precious yeast. The yeast was in little wrapped moist cakes of greeny-gray yellow. They lived in a brown glass jar in the darkest part of the cupboard. Like a little mouse at the cheese I sometimes had a surreptitious nibble of one of the two cakes we used each time. I didn't much like the taste and it made my mouth pucker but I still nibbled away anyway. The two yeast cakes were crumbled into the milk along with a dollop of sugar, the whole was given a stir and set to keep warm on the end of the stove away from the fire over the hot water reservoir. The sack of flour, a peck I think, was dragged out of its corner, across the lino and set handy by, while cupfuls flew into the bowl and sprinkled themselves around the place. The final ingredients were some butter scooped up on two big fingers or one little hand and 'not too much' salt.

At last all was ready and the first mixing began. Big hands worn and creased, together with little hands, clean for the occasion, first of all stirred the dry mountains of flour into patterns just for the fun of it. Then in went the milk mixture, pale yellow-gray from the yeast, bubbled into froth, just warm to touch and smelling strongly of fermentation. Puddles of it gathered and were mixed into the flour mountains until the whole became a glorious sticky elastic mess. Then more flour, thrown in with ardor, mixed again. Then a bit more milk mixture - "always save some" - flour again, until big hands and little hands were stuck together in messy confusion.

Then more flour on the bottom of the bowl as the dough was lifted first one side and then the other. The rhythm took over. The lifting and pulling and rolling followed the soft lump on its journey first onto the floured table and soon disentangled little hands which then rested on top of big hands as the ritual gained momentum until the whole sticky mass became a solid soft cushion covered in flour. Then back into the bowl again to sit exactly where it should in the center of its own round world. Just like Mama. I wiped my hands down my front, just like Mama, as the cheesecloth was placed over the dough and the bowl replaced the milk pan on the cool side of the stove.

Then we were happy. Mama made tea in her special pot with the long spout. I might have cocoa again or maybe "chamomile tea". It was years before I learned that chamomile tea was not just milk and hot water and sugar. In summer we might go out into the dooryard. There to sit in the sunshine or else I might go off about my business. Oh, the disappointment if I didn't hear her call to the next part of the dance. This time we didn't bother with aprons but plunged hands into the flour bag and then, with stiff probing fingers prodded the now swollen belly in the bowl to reduce it, hissing and popping, to a flat but pox-marked shapeless mass until, once more the rhythm took over and restored anew the round plump pillow, more smooth now and slightly glistening on the top, in place once again in the flour lined bowl on the cool side of the stove.Then a long wait.

At last it was time to don aprons again. By now Mama's mood was apparent. Sometimes she sang as she dusted the table with handfuls of flour expertly fanned to sprinkle the whole area needed.

Sometimes she was quiet with set features. She was never neutral. The rhythm of the next quadrille was established. The initial ritual never varied. First the now fully risen dough was turned out of its resting place. Long sticky tentacles tried to hold it back but they never succeeded. Mama was much too powerful. There it rested, upside down in the middle of the white expanse as vulnerable as a pubescent child.

This next part never included me. I was spectator. First the great mass was turned in upon itself, rolled and stretched and forced inward again and again. Those powerful hands worked with a sure knowledge, silently reducing the whole to elastic, a live springy ball with a life of its own. It rolled this way and that. It was turned and slapped and thrown onto the table sometimes with singing and sometimes with vengeance until it lay silent and quivering in a cowering mound against the white. Now, Mama always stopped and wiped her hands down her apron before she took up the butcher knife and cut the dough cleanly in half with one quick swipe.

The raw glistening edges of each half were then turned in like a navel and the whole process of rolling and kneading began again upon each twin in turn. Then each of the two were cut and shaped again until there were four rounds of dough in a line on the table. They had a rest then, Mama and the four lumps of dough.

After a little while Mama began again and cut one round in half, one into twenty-four small pieces and left the other two big. Then it was my turn. While Mama worked upon the others shaping two large loves and two small ones, I was given, one by one, small bits to make into little rounds, I had to work so, so carefully "just like this" and place the little blobs each beside each in the flat tin like twelve babies in a bed - four rows of three - "not too close; they need to breathe". Then I started on the other tin. Sometimes if I was slow or careless Mama would finish off my 'babies'.

One day I began to bawl and holler because there were only twelve babies. "Where am I? I'm not there!" Without a word Mama cut off a piece of dough from the end of her loaf and efficiently and expertly fashioned it into a round and "shifted everybody over" to make room in the tin for a 'Baker's dozen'. After that our tins always had an uneven look with thirteen buns.

Occasionally, if it was a singing day or an especially angry day, Mama and I would take one lot of small pieces and add cinnamon, sugar and raisins to them - then we had thirteen cinnamon buns. Sometimes, very rarely, she magically transfigured them into all sorts of shapes twisted and braided, or with two ears and a fat tummy. This menagerie was then lined up in the tin, covered with melted butter and sugar sprinkled on each; most usually though they were just sweet cinnamon versions of my rolls. When all of this kneading and shaping was finished, the tins were put to prove on the cool side of the stove where each tin jostled for space. The mounds had their tops oiled with melted butter and were left exposed like so many bottoms in a row. I seldom seemed to be around when the pans were maneuvered into the oven, on three tiers, a big loaf and a small one side by side on the top and middle rack and the two flat bun tins side by side on the bottom. A rotation took place sometime and the tins of buns always ended up on the top shelf. Depending on the time of year, the fire and how the wind was blowing the bread came out pale, or dark or middling. Sometimes disaster struck and my buns had black bottoms or tops with very black raisins. Or maybe, a loaf might be dark along one side. But - the smell never varied and there are no words to describe it.

When they came out of the oven the loaves were turned out of their tins onto their sides. A knock on the bottom, which sounded hollow, meant they were done. Sometimes they had to be put back again for "just a few minutes". When they were at last ready the tops were greased again with butter and they were set to cool. Again, the table, by this time cleaned of flour and covered with a piece of sheet was the center of attention as it received the offering. I wondered if I had been put on the table after my turn in the oven to be admired and exclaimed over.

There is no taste in the world like newly baked bread. Contentment was sitting beside Mama before the others came home "just sampling" one of my little rolls - "not too much because hot bread gives you the collywobbles".

Chapter Seven

Cats, Frogs and Chickens

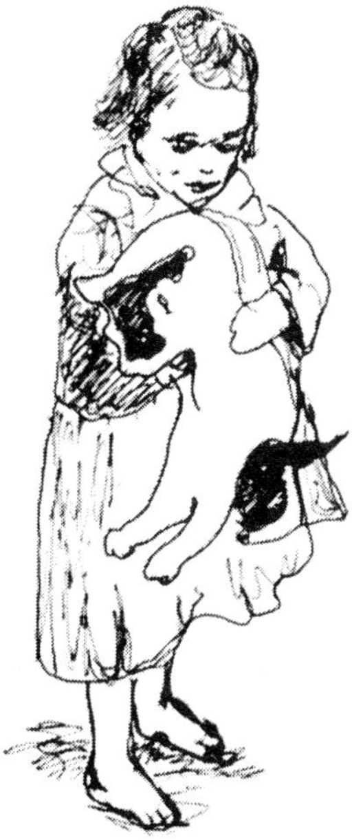

In the years before I started school season followed season in an endless seam. I was mostly at home alone with Mama once Jimmy had joined the others on their walk to school. I had my dolls to keep me company and we spent our time well. But I had other companions not all of them imaginary. There was usually a dog that followed me everywhere. The one I remember best was called Skippy. We didn't bother too much about each other except he tagged along. My real friends were the chickens and Tippy the cat. She was large, independent and she loved me. She purred back and forth across my legs if she wanted my attention; she knew how to get away if she didn't want to be bothered with my games.

Tippy, contrary to most people's opinion of cats, liked the water.

On a bright early morning she could often be found playing with her shadow in a puddle. But her favorite pastime was to go down to the brook and play along the edges trying to catch grasshoppers and dragonflies. She never did. She would sit with infinite patience on a stone near the shallows staring into the bottom with great concentration for endless minutes. I used to sneak up on her and try to find out what she saw but I never found anything remarkable in the place where she stared. Maybe cats see things we don't.

Tippy had an aptitude for catching frogs, which she seemed convinced that I wanted. Tippy would appear up at the house with a frog in her mouth. It was always alive and seldom injured. She would put it down at my feet with one paw on top and look up expectantly; it was clearly a gift for me. If the frog managed to get away, Tippy would chase it and stop it with a paw, or else, worry and tease it until I intervened. Time and time again I explained that frogs lived near

the water and they didn't like to be petted. I had to take them back and set them free near the water. One day, in exasperation, I carried Tippy down under my arm whilst clutching the frog with two hands to let it go in the brook. Then, standing knee deep, I lectured Tippy on the facts of life about frogs and cats. Frogs ought to go in the water; cats ought not to. She didn't listen, gave a squirm and jumped nearly to the bank, landed with her back legs in the water and went, as if chased by a witch, up to the house to clean herself in some secluded corner. The next day back she was with another frog dangling through her whiskers.

One morning Pop went rushing after Tippy and took the frog from her. "Go get some more you damned fool cat and we'll have a mess of them for breakfast".

"You can't eat frogs", I told him

"They eat them all the time in France. You wait and see." He took the poor frog and cut off its legs with one quick swipe. He got out the frying pan and set it to heat on the stove, skinned off the green skin and exposed the whitish green flesh and when the pan was smoking hot he put them in to sizzle. A pair of pink hued breeches curled with the heat and seemed to jump themselves out onto a plate. Well used to cooking fish that had just been caught and chickens that had been running around the dooryard a few hours before they became roasted and squirrels dropped to the ground by a shotgun, my curiosity overcame any feeling for the frog. I thought it tasted of nothing much except hot butter and salt and pepper and a twinge of regret. Us kids then went through a phase of competing with Tippy for frogs so Pop could have a mess of them for breakfast now and then. He seemed to like them.

Frogs couldn't jump once they had been cut in half but a fascination about chickens was the way in which they could run around for several seconds once their heads had been removed. Two were killed nearly every Sunday and it was my big brothers' job to do it. But it was usually my job to catch them as I was good at it and the chickens knew me. We put them in a burlap bag and swung them round for a bit to daze them and then chopped off the head with a quick cut of the axe. Then they were put down to run around spurting blood all over. It was a kind of blood sport and we didn't think it cruel. It made the chopping off of the head easier to contemplate. Once dead the chickens were still warm and had to be hung up by their legs to drip before being plucked, gutted and made ready for the pot.

Mama cooked the chickens in a big pot on the stove. We had them for Sunday dinner always when the older boys were still home before the war. They simmered for hours on the back of the range. I loved pot liquour. Mama let me stand on a chair and dip a piece of bread in the juice, down through the yellow into the pot and straight into my mouth so the yellow bits ran down my chin. She often made dumplings out of flour dough and I could stand on the chair and lower them into the pot to float above the chicken as they cooked.

The chickens and I had a love/hate relationship. Mostly they were my friends and it was my job to let them out in the morning to run and scratch about. But occasionally one would stray too far and then I must spend a lot of time running about after the squawking critter to try and get it home. In the winter time they only came out for a little while in the middle of the day and had to be shut in again in the early afternoon.

On one cold day in early winter before the others had come home from school I went down to get some wood for Mama. I saw the chickens waiting to be let back into the coop; the door had blown shut. They were huddled together and went inside willingly.

I was proud of the amount of wood I could carry. You stick out one arm as far as you can to make a shelf. Then you carefully lay the split logs along it one by one in a neat row putting another row on the first until you have an armful so big you can hardly see over the top. Then you stagger back up to the house to let the whole lot drop into the wood box still in their neat rows. This day I had the biggest load I could carry and I was making my way up the frosty path when I saw the rooster. He was the biggest, white one, the king of the coop.

He was sitting on a stone in the middle of the steepest part of the way up to the house. His red comb bobbed about as he watched me try to pass him. His black eye peered and followed mine. His yellow beak made little sharp jabs at the air.

You get away from me. Go! Shoo!

He paid me no mind. I tried to run up the bank over a grassy bit and slipped down on my back with my armful of wood clutched tightly. The rooster jumped up onto the wood and then onto me.

His yellow claws scratched a hold on my chest as they kneaded firmly down. His eye looked down into mine. He began to peck my face. I knew that roosters could eat out your eyes. Peck, he came, peck, closer and closer to my eyes as I twisted my face back and forth too terrified to even scream. Nobody came to get me. He stayed there making quick darts towards my face with his neck stretching out and his waddles quivering, his eye on mine. I don't remember how I got away. I remember the sticks of wood scattered across the pathway. I remember arriving at the house with bloody scratches on my face, snot on my sleeve and my armful of wood reduced to just enough sticks to save the fire, incoherent with sobs and indignation.

Hens were much safer. It is quite friendly to squat down beside a hen while she keeps her eggs warm. Broody hens sometimes make nests in the most unlikely places. One made her nest under the metal wayside sign we used as a toboggan in winter, which was then abandoned in the long grass on the hillside where we

made the snow run. She didn't seem to mind me sitting with her as she hatched away at her eggs. We clucked at each other. I brought her bread and corn. Only two hatched into yellow 'peepers'. The other cold eggs lay abandoned in the nest beside the slimy, cracked eggshells of the two newborn chicks. I finally smashed them against the stonewall in a stinking ritual of destruction.

Usually the chickens were content to scratch away in the dooryard or in the long grass, flocking together only when feeding time came in the morning and evening. One summer they began to gather under the kitchen window at breakfast time. Each day I kneeled up at the window with my bowl of lumpy, gray oatmeal swimming in yesterday's 'gone off' milk. When nobody was looking I dumped my breakfast out and watched them fight and scramble to get their share.

"What in the hell are those chickens doing squawking their heads off every day?" Pop wanted to know.

I dunno. It ain't my fault if they wanna.

As well as being a good catcher of frogs Tippy was good at having kittens. Once she had them on the seat behind the kitchen range. There was one Rinkie loved more than the others. He was small and grey with a tail that stuck out like a nail. She called him Spikey. The rest of the litter disappeared one night but Spikey was allowed to live. It was wintertime and he became a constant companion. Usually she knew exactly where he was all of the time. But one night she was too busy trying to stay up past her bedtime to remember Spikey.

Cold came in through the closed windows, through the dark night, through the far away talk in the warm kitchen. The kitchen was even warmer because the bedroom door was tightly closed tonight to keep the light and laughter shut out. She was excluded. She had been put to bed long ago and Mama had finished all of her stories and songs and was out having a cup of tea. Rinkie had been out three or four times for a drink, to say she was cold, just to look, slip into the circle of light around the table and hope they wouldn't notice that she had sneaked out to join them again.

Now she was back, back in bed. Somebody had warmed up a flat iron and wrapped it in newspaper to put down near her feet. She had the sheet and feather bed pulled up around her neck so just her mouth poked out and her eyes. She could nearly see how her breath must look in the cold with plumes of white like the words in the 'Katz and Jammers' mouths in the Funnies. She could nearly see the white frost feathers on the windows. The feather bed was just beginning to feel as warm as it had before Mama got out. The cold edges were a bit further away. She might go to sleep and began to sing in a low voice so nobody would hear.

Jackie Frost, Jackie Frost came in the night.
Left the meadows that he crossed
All gleaming white.

What was that? Somebody singing? A baby crying out in the cold? The Little Match Girl trying to sell matches?

She listened.

There it went again, a tiny cry in the night - a sort of mewing. She got up again, bare feet hitting the cold boards. At the window she could see the moonlight reflected on the bank beside the pathway. She could see the Jackie Frost patterns on the windowpane. Through the frosty glass she could just see Spikey, her grey kitten with a tail like a big nail; it was straight and came to a point on the end. He was Tippy's latest baby, the only one they had been allowed to keep. Spikey saw her and jumped up on the sill and mewed louder and scratched at the glass.

Rinkie tried to open the window but it was stuck down with ice. She didn't know what to do. If they were still in the kitchen they might just shout and send her back to bed. She opened the door a crack. The kitchen was empty; the lamp was gone from the middle of the table. It was dark with only the glow from the stove where fire lit up the cracks around the grate and under the stove lids. Some moonlight came slanting in.

They must be in the other room.

She went out into the warm kitchen. She could see, at the far side, the shut door with the light around the edges.

They are in the other room, with both lamps and the pot-bellied stove hot all the way round. Pop is reading out loud.

She felt her way to the backdoor and opened it. A blast of cold pushed into her. Spikey was nowhere to be seen. Out she went with her bare feet feeling the sharp ground. She crept along, close to the house calling:

Spikey. I'm here. Come puss, puss, puss. Here Kitty, kitty, kitty-

She was just past the kitchen's second window when the little furry ball came knocking into her legs.

Oh Spikey are you cold? Did you get shut out, you poor little thing? Come to bed. You should have been in bed long ago. You are a naughty thing. Come and get warm beside me.

For a change Spikey did not struggle as Rinkie carried him back, carefully shutting the doors behind her. When she got back to bed it still had a warm place on her side of it, next to the wall to leave room for Mama when she came back. She snuggled down in the Rinkie sized dent in the feather bed. Her feet carefully reached down to the hot iron that now felt hotter than ever on her icy feet. Spikey settled down to purr beside her head.

I love little kitty
Her coat is so warm
And if I don't hurt her
She'll do me no harm.

So I'll not pull her tail
Or drive her away
But kitty and I
Very gently will play.

You're a he aren't you Spikey? So I'll not pull his tail – his spikey nail tail. Go under the covers Spikey, its warmer in there.

They were soon asleep. It must have been one of the nights when Mama slept in with Pop because when morning came Rinkie was still alone in the bed and there was no warm place when Mama had been. She stretched out her toes and could feel the cracking newspaper around the now stone cold iron.

What's that?

She could feel a furry thing beside the iron. She burrowed down to the bottom of the bed. She took out Spikey all stiff and truly dead. His normally straight tail hanging down and his teeth showing in a bad dream grin.

I didn't want him to freeze in the cold. I wanted him to be warm beside me.

Mama clucked and held her on her lap as she sobbed. Spikey was now lain out on the table. Mama crooned, 'Never mind. Never mind.' But she did mind forever and ever.

Chapter Eight

Sugaring Off

Today is the day the sap begins to run up the trees.

Old snow still clings to the stone wall fence, dirty grey snow riddled with holes and black spots. A ring of melting ice is all that is left of the snow house we made in the roadside drifts from the last big storm. Mud slipped me up as I ran down the driveway, clanging the tin cans together.

Wait for me. Wait for me.

This song echoed through the years.

I'm coming, wait for me!

The big boys were at the end of the drive with knives, a hatchet and the brace-and-bit. Jimmy got there first and clanged his load of cans down in a heap. I put mine carefully one by one. How did they know it was today? I counted the line of Maple trees that marched along the drive and then down onto the road.

There must be a hundred to do.

Naw – only about twelve maybe thirteen.

There's got to be thirteen.

Shut up and go and get some more.

I kicked my way back to the cellar. How did they know it was the right day?

Carl, how do you know?

It just is; you'll have to take my word for it.

We'd already got the wood for the spigots, days ago. So they must have known we'd need it soon. But how did they know?

It must be something the sunbeams tell them in the misty morning, or maybe the birds getting worms out of the puddles, or the chickens going broody. Whatever it was, we ran out to meet it, slithering in mud and old snow with the promise of candy in the air.

You start by making the spigots. Short pieces of green wood, hollow wood like willow or elder, about the thickness of Carl's thumb and about four times as long were what they needed. It was exactly the same kind of wood Jiggy used to make us whistles when he teased the bark off one end, cut a small flat trough and then a hole into the hollow middle and slipped the bark back with a sharpened mouth piece. Jimmy and me, we were the experts at finding just the right stems from down by the brook where we made our bows and arrows.

Jimmy and I might be blowing our wooden whistles while Carl and Benny made spigots. They whistled a much better tune that our one note toots as they whittled the sticks down to a sharp point on one end. If there was not already a channel, a groove was cut, in any case on the opposite end the side was flattened and a wedge slanted downward to allow the sap to run down the grove and drip off the end. When they had enough, you needed extras in case some split, we were sent to fetch the brace-and-bit. One of the big kids drilled a hole in each tree, another drove home the tap, us little kids were in charge of the collecting pails.

These were big tin cans. The biggest ones Pop brought home from someplace or other; the rest had held canned foods from Honon's Store. To make them into buckets Pop made wire handles. They were saved down in the cellar. We had to go into the dark to get them. They were always rusting, dirty and sometimes had holes and spiders. We clanged our way down the driveway kicking a rusty one or two along in front.

"You kids go and get them washed". So we pounded our way down the road to the brook where we spent a wet time sloshing water at each other and then ran back up the hill.

"Did you test them? I'll bet you didn't test them". Back down to the brook to fill them one by one to see if they leaked. The ones that did had to be mended with a washer and a nut and bolt. The new ones Pop had made that winter were always the best shiny ones and never leaked. The really rusty ones had to be junked. Finally we had them all lined up ready to go. Once Jimmy took out his pecker and pissed in every one. "Damn you kids; go and wash them again".

Tapping the trees took nearly the whole of one day. The hole had to be drilled in about two feet from the ground. The spigot driven in with sharp true hammer blows so as not to damage or split it, a big nail just above and then the pail hung on the nail. If we were lucky the sap started to drip right away. Most trees would give a few drips as soon as they were tapped but it was the next day, or more, before we could begin to fill the vat in which it was to be simmered. This stood ready on the back of the kitchen range. Once the pails were hanging in place you just had to wait.

Carl was the expert candy maker.

'When we gonna make the candy?

We ain't got enough yet. We need tons more. Besides there isn't any snow.

Why do we need snow? Can't we just make fudge?

Taffey is better; we need snow. Now scram.

At first we waited impatiently for the sap to drip the pail full enough to be emptied; the first day we watched it all day long and proudly took a pail with a few inches in the bottom up to the house but as the few weeks of collecting drew on we were less attentive. The warmer the day the faster it dripped, on a cold day it might not run at all. In the early morning, on the way to school, Jimmy and I could often lick a sweet icicle broken from the spigot. Some mornings the pails were solid with sweet ice. If the day was hot, like sometimes in March, we might be busy all day running to empty the pails before they ran over. We got home from school earlier than the big kids who went on the bus. So it was often our job to rescue a brim full pail and get it into the house without spilling.

I could stand, knees bent, with my mouth on a tap drinking sweet water from the tree. Or lying under it as the sap dripped into my open mouth, washing my face, making sweet tears on my cheeks.

We put the sap into a big pan; I suppose it must have been a jelly pan, on the back of the kitchen range. There it slowly simmered into maple syrup.

It's snowing Carl. Look it's snowing. Can we do it? Can we make it?

OK. We'll have a sugaring off. Just like they used to in the old days. Go and get some more wood.

But it's dark.

You can take the lantern. The fire needs to be hot to boil the syrup into candy.

Jimmy, Halcie and I went out into the dark with the lantern swinging and smoking up its globe as we made footprints in the late snow down to the woodpile and back. We might meet Billy coming back from milking the cow; the job fell to him when Johnny wasn't around.

'Carl's going to sugar–off tonight!'

Then don't trample the snow all up you little sap.

Why? I'm making the last snow angel.

Don't! We need clean snow, not used snow for sugaring off.

The lantern cast a wavy shadow as I carried it back because the boys had their arms full of wood. I couldn't help running into the new snow this way and that, back and forth.

You're spoiling it you little sap

I'm just using up a little bit.

Carl won't do it if you use up all the good snow.

We stamped our feet at the door. Carl had some syrup in the pan Mama boiled chickens in. He made up the fire with some

of our wet wood, which sizzled and sung as it dried out. He had the lid off so the flames came up around the pan. I stood on a chair and watched him stir. After a long time he put the lid back on the stove and pulled the pan to one side.

Now it's just gotta boil undisturbed.

Why?

Because it does. Go in the other room and play buzz.

I joined the others in the other room around the potbellied stove there. They were playing 'Can you top this?' Each one was telling a joke trying to 'top' the one before like on the radio. Even Pop joined in; it was one of his favourite games.

My turn. What's black and white and red all over?

That's the oldest joke in the universe. A newspaper.

Ahhhhh. Knock, knock.

Who's there?

I dunno.

That's not a joke. Go away.

I went back to the kitchen to see how Carl was getting on. He sent me outside to get a plate full of snow. He carefully drizzled boiling syrup onto the snow. It wasn't ready yet. Carl and I ate it anyway even if it was just a gooey mess.

Ooie Gooey was a worm

A mighty worm was he.

He sat upon the railroad track

The train he did not see

OOOOie Gooooeeyy

We watched it boil some more and I got another plate of snow. The next time we tried it, it 'cracked' when it hit the snow.

That's it! Go and get the others. Here she blows.

We stood around protecting a clean patch of snow as Carl came with the pan and twisted a pattern of hot syrup in front of us. There is no time to deliberate about what the patterns will be, but they are always twisted in hurried convolutions. The last bit may twist up in a pointed stalagmite from the depths of the snow to echo the stalactites hanging from the taps all down the line of maple trees. That is if you are lucky and have the right combination of snow, cold, sugar mixture and quickness of hand. Carl did. The brown curly patterns seared deep into the white, the only trace on the snow surface was a curved hole with yellow ochre stained edges. By magic it cut a yellow hole into the snow and when we dared to touch it, it was hard and not even sticky but had turned into real maple taffy with a bit of ice frozen into the bottom and maybe a little grass too. The next morning the snow had melted into just a memory of amber stains and sweet maple candy.

The sap continued for a little while until it was time to take out the spigots, ram in a plug to heal the scar, put the buckets in the cellar and wait for next year. The maple syrup that didn't get used on pancakes or oatmeal was bottled in old ketchup or sauce bottles, capped and put away upstairs on an old table, rows and rows of bottled sunshine. They grew dusty as summer came. The sun made the amber liquid dance against the wall and shine in long ribbons of light to make the dust particles dance. Watching the sun play with those amber people standing in rows was my first conscious memory of beauty. It had no name or words. It was colour and light. It was me and not me; me outside and inside myself; but also inside the amber sweetness. I guess it could be named happiness, the oneness of the breast.

Chapter Nine

A Ticking Clock

At the end of our lane, just where the road curved to go off to Newtown, stood Mrs.MacArthur's house. It was a typical New England farmhouse. It was big, white shingled, had a porch all across the front and to one side, a long lawn which ended in a bank beside the road, and, both an outdoor pump for water and another in the scullery sink. Long before I was born our family lived there for a time. There used to be a Mr.MacArthur but one Christmas Day he was out in the cold cranking his car to get it started to go to church and he fell over dead in the snow. Of course I don't really remember it as it happened long before me but every time the story was told I could see him in his hat like Abraham Lincoln's lying out under the car, a black post fallen over in the snow.

Mrs.MacArthur was my friend. I went to visit her to listen to her clock ticking. She was small, bent, white haired and wore old-fashioned neat clothes. Her shoes were black with laces and her feet were pressed close together to keep her knees up. Her hands wrinkled down the backs and her face wrinkled all over. I was small, dirty, barefoot and ragged but we liked each other.

I would arrive, usually clutching some small offering. Mama said we had to be nice to Mrs.MacArthur. She always answered my knock with a quiet nod of her head and the beginning of a smile. She had hard candy in a dish on the table but that was for later. We would sit opposite each other in the quiet. She had two clocks. One was a large Grandfather clock which didn't work. It had a silver face covered with pictures of the moon, sun, stars and curly-cues in gold. It had numbers in black spider writing. There was another one, smaller but big enough to stand by itself, had a clear white face and Roman numbers. This was the one that ticked.

I never much talked to Mrs.MacArthur nor she to me. We sat there, she in her rocking chair and me in a black wooden armchair with my dusty feet clenched on the bottom rung in the front. We mostly listened – to the clock ticking very loud in the stillness – or to the wind blowing – or just to our own breathing. I learned, with no teacher except Mrs.MacArthur's two clocks, the Roman numbers up to twelve.

Sometimes she would go out to the kitchen and pump up some water and make us tea – real tea with milk and sugar and sometimes cakes served on a tray with a lacy cloth all newly ironed. Her floor was made of black and white tiles like the chequers board at home. I would sit and watch them. When I looked at them long enough they began to move and dance until I nearly fell off the chair trying to keep up with them. When she went out to make the tea I sometimes walked on all of the white squares and sometimes on the black ones or tried a little hopscotch. But mostly I just sat and listened and looked. It was a place of peace where I could feel myself full of me. I never knew what she thought about.

In the spring I always took her the first bunch of spring flowers. At first Tonie went with me on our way home from Bakey's field. Tonie took me flower picking every spring. On just the right day we would go off up to Bakey's hill and into Bakey's field.

Are we goin' flower pickin'?

No.

Why?

'Cause they ain't ready yet?

Ohhhhhhhh.

Okay we'll try.

See I tol ya they weren't ready yet. I'LL tell you when we can go. You gotta wait for the right day!

The flowers were always there on the day we were sure spring had come. The day that smelled right and felt right - the right day. When the birds sang to each other and the sun twinkled through new blades of grass. They were never there if we chanced it too soon. On the first day there might only be violets, blue ones and white ones and , if we were lucky, yellow ones. There might be blood root, white flowers that wept tears of blood when picked. Maybe cowslips down near the swamp. But in the next weeks there were sure to be the tiny stars of hepatica, wood anemone like snow-white angels, Johnny-jump-ups, trilliums and some we called 'wake robins' with wide open bird mouths. If we searched long and hard there were Jack-in-the Pulpit growing under the tallest trees. Tonie left home when I was about seven so then I went picking flowers on my own.

Mama got most of them to put in a jelly glass on the table. She would hold them up to her nose and smell them smiling all the time. But Mrs.MacArthur also always received hers with joy. She couldn't walk far. She put them in a vase and sat and looked at them while I looked and listened to the silence surrounding the clock's ticking. After a time I would unwind my feet and tell her I had to go. That was her cue to offer me a candy from the dish and sometimes a few pennies. Out I rushed, away from the quietness, whooping and shouting and running full pelt the half mile to Honon's store to take a long time choosing my penny worth of candy from the big glass case.

Sometimes I cheated. I would raid Mrs MacArthur's own bank of myrtle and arrive at her door with a fist full of her own flowers. She never let on that she knew where they came from; she even seemed grateful and put them in the same little vase. But I knew. I never stayed so long, nor took tea, nor listened to the clock ticking. I stood on one foot and waited for a penny then just took it and ran; alive, still full of my own self but without the feeling of belonging, of being and becoming, not renewed by the ticking clock, shared silence and dancing black and white squares.

Chapter Ten

Marbles and Fishing

Usually Jimmy and I were, sort of, good friends. We played together in the dooryard digging in the dirt and worked on the elaborate system of tunnels and fortifications that made up a small town. We went off on the run to chase behind the two wheeled 'fire-putter-outer' that the family had acquired. It was a large red water tank on two wheels with shafts in the front. I think it was meant to be horse drawn but we raced about with it bumping along the dirt track as some kind of war chariot. We laughed and ran and fought our way through the sunny days.

There was one day when we were fighting and complaining about each other so much, Ma decided to take action. She made us clean the kitchen windows. We had vinegar and water on cloths to wash and then wads of scrunched up newspaper to polish them off. Ma put us one inside and one outside and we had to clean both sides of the window at the same time. It was soon a game of mimic and laughter. We made it last long after all the bottoms of the windows were clean; we couldn't reach the top ones. We were soaked through with laughter and vinegar water and silly faces.

When she forced us to stop, she had a new suggestion. 'Why don't you go and play marbles?'

It ain't time yet.

Yah. Nobody's playing marbles. Marbles are sissy.

She just ignored our protests and got them out anyway. We spent a long time sorting them. We had a large and most beautifully interesting collection. There were 'biggies' and 'littlies', 'giants' and 'tinies' with a few 'gargantuan' and 'pee-wees'. There were 'glassies' both plain and shot, coloured or colourless with veins and swirls, 'stonies' which were heavy plain coloured in milky hues and, most prized of all 'aggies' with beautifully veined marking, no two the same. How wealthy we were with these magical playthings- wonderful orbs of character and beauty – worlds to hold in our hands, capsules of dreams.

As if by magic, that was the day marble season started. When we ran off to find Danny he had his marbles too. Without consultation the marble season arrives when it is Time and not one day before. This year I was going to be counted in.

There were undefined demarcations in those of us eligible to play marbles in any given year. It was something to do with age and sex coupled with sophistication and desire. Always before, depending upon how many brothers were currently in the marble brigade, I made up my cloth bagful, or barely less than empty, out of the leftovers and the ones that began to roll out from odd jars, tins, cracks and crevices about the house and barn. I was never before eligible to play. I was the runt and a girl. But I always managed to fight my way into a share of the baubles and to convince one or two of my brothers that I could be a useful practice partner.

They played for 'keepsies' in the neighbourhood games but I would never consent to lose any of my hard fought for loot. I increased my stock by having a keen eye to seek them out from where they had been hiding in dark corners for the year past or by noticing them where they accidentally rolled in the far reaches of the dooryard or along the road. Sometimes I could make a good trade if I successfully challenged somebody with one of those rare marbles that, by itself, knew how to beat all comers. Or I might steal them from somebody who had so many there was no danger of being caught. At the end of the season they all went back in a big wooden drum to be fought over and coveted again next year. Sometimes, on solitary winter afternoons, I would seek out the marble store and play at trains rolling them round the inside of a pot lid or make up games where they rolled down cardboard or wooden planks or dropped onto small catapults to shoot over cardboard cut-outs. But that was not real marbles. Real marbles had a very short spring. Now I was part of it. How did Ma know the right day had come? It must have been because the windows were clean.

In between marbles and swimming came fishing.

'Let's go fishin'.

Yah – let's. We need poles an' worms an' hooks an' string.

We're goin' fishin'.

The older boys had already cut new fishing poles. We knew where they were hidden. They were down behind the barn. Long and straight and really bendy with lots of 'give' so they wouldn't snap. They cut new ones every year. There were lots of sizes of just the right thickness and length to suite each fisherman – and me. I was barely tolerated as 'tag along' with the older boys but so was Jimmy. We were too noisy and fickle to be serious fishers. We often went off together, companion and friend for the time being anyway.

Our fishing gear was uncomplicated. The poles had a grove cut round the top into which the string was tied. About two feet from the bottom end we tied a lead sinker and at the very end the hook. Sometimes we had a piece of cork tied a couple of feet above the sinker. This cork 'bobber' was to float on the water to tell us if we had a bite. It was not essential. What was necessary was some kind of bait. To collect worms for fishing you needed either a jar with a screw down lid or, better still a can with a lid.

You get the cocoa can.

No you…

You..

OK… but then I get to put the holes in. You get the dirt.

Once we had the can ready we could begin to collect worms. We started off by turning over stones.

Hey lookie here.

Hundreds. They must be babies – look how little and squirmy.

They ain't no good – ya need biggies to catch fish.

We'll take some just in case....

We soon tired of looking under stones to find only tiny pale excuses for worms. We wanted big fat ones. The best place to dig for them was in the garden because the ground was soft there. Jimmy used the shovel and I got on my hands and knees and dug; we found plenty of fat worms. Digging in the garden was not allowed once things had been planted but nobody knew; we carefully patted it down afterward. We were not found out until much later when beans, carrots and peas came up all in a muddle in one small spot.

It must have been the dog. He's always digging in there.

Once the can was full enough we had time to cut a few worms in half so they could make two.

Did you know that if you cut a worm in half it grows again into two worms?

From both ends?

Yah – so next time we'll get double.

We always collected lots and lots of worms because we planned to catch enough fish for a 'mess' for supper. It didn't dawn on us that we always had about three-quarters of a can-full too many.

The other essential thing was a small 'v' shaped stick with one short leg. The short leg was sharpened to a fine point. This was to bring home the fish with the point sticking through its mouth and then out through one gill. We wanted to catch a brook or rainbow trout but mostly the fish were catfish. Nobody except the cat ate them and I thought that was where their name came from but Jimmy told me it was because of their whiskers and spiny fin on the head. We didn't eat them because they didn't taste good.

Pop don't like them. Fit only for the cat. Throw it back.

Jimmy and I usually did a lot of moving about when we fished. We might start down at the small bridge in front of the house, sitting up on the edge with our feet dangling over. Nobody had ever caught a fish there that we knew of but it was the quickest place to get to and, I suppose, the only place we were allowed to go at first.

We sat side by side with the worm can perched between us, treading our worms onto the hook. It was a sticky business.

Ooooie goooy was a worm

A mighty worm was he

He sat upon the railway track

The train he did not see.

Ooooooie Gooooooie.

When the hooks were baited we dangled in the lines and watched them being carried away downstream. The fast current at this bridge caused lots of throbs and tugs that seemed like fish biting but never were. Often after our lines were tangled a time or two we hauled them in and went someplace else. When we were small it was just to another spot along the brook near

our road but as we got older it was to the swimming hole, or back upstream to Bakey's Bridge on the tarred road past the swimming hole. When we were older still it was to Terrill's Bridge on the main road where the brook became a river, deep and not too swift. Some mornings would find us fishing at every place fish were known to bite and some places, like the small bridge, where they weren't.

Mostly we didn't catch much and if we did get one it was likely to be a cat-fish or else too small to keep. They had to be at least six inches long to be eligible for the frying pan but, oh, the joy when the line tightened, dipped down and, when jerked in, it had a wriggling slapping fish on the end no matter how small or what variety. Once, and only once, I caught a real wopper.

It was an early spring day with a slanting sun just visible through the mists of morning. We went first to the little bridge but didn't even bother to put on bait. Without discussion we turned and ran up the hill and down the tarred road to the swimming hole. After a bit of argument about who would fish where, Jimmy settled on the diving board and I chose the bank beside the shallows. By now the sun was up and hot on my back. It fell across the water turning its black water into soft browns, yellows and greens as it played with the ripples.

The water plonked and sent out circles when my sinker hit the surface and the hook, half covered with still wriggling worm, sank slowly bottom-ward. I waited and watched more patiently than many times. The sides of the pond were alive with insect activity. I could see snake spit on the grass blades and I noticed how smooth the muddy bank was except for the little piles of earth where some creature had dug holes the size of nickels. The water that now and again kissed my bare feet was cold. It was too early for swimming; that's why we were fishing.

A bird came down and took a piece of twig from very near me. I thought it wanted my worms but it was nests it was interested in, not food for nesters, as might have been the case in a few weeks. As I watched, unthinking, my pole began to vibrate a bit. Then the line began to jerk. I was tempted to pull it in but decided it was only a nibble. Soon it happened again – and again. Then the line pulled tight and the end of my pole dipped.

I've got one. I've got one.

Jimmy came leaping off the diving board down to the bank. Together we pulled it out. Me running backward up the bank and Jimmy holding the line and pulling hand over hand. Then he jerked it quickly and a ten-inch brown trout landed flipping at my feet. It nearly got back into the water. Hampered by our excitement, we had trouble grabbing hold of it and I fell into the shallows. Finally, Jimmy got it with both hands and I tried to insert the pointed stick. At last I got it speared and took the hook from it's bloodied mouth. Then we ran yelling all of the way home.

Rinkie's got one. She's caught a big 'un.

I've got one. I've got one.

Somebody helped us gut it and Mama fried it there and then - all golden in butter, crisp at the edges with flour and salt and pepper. Unspeakable joy. After that, fishing never quite held the same charm. The anticipated disappointment was too great.

Chapter Eleven

The Swimming Hole

Water flowed through our summertime as the sap rose up the trees in spring. Mostly we went swimming everyday – all day or two or three times in a day but everyday. My early childhood ended just before I went back to the swimming hole one August day in 1944. That, however, comes later.

The swimming hole was about half a mile away from our house. It was formed by a widening out of the brook as it poured under a disused bridge. It was the nerve centre of summer, used by generations of kids in Hawleyville. My sister, Tonie, remembers taking me for the first time one hot summer day when I was only nine or ten months old and she was just coming up for eleven years.

To get there we went down the lane and along the road past Mrs.MacArthur's, turned sharp right down the main tarred road away from the village and then turned left into what had been a railroad track. Now it was an overgrown lane ending in a sand basin about as big as a beach in a small cove, which, in turn, ended abruptly at the steep drop of a former train bridge. There was no way across the bridge to the other side, just the sheer wall into the shallow rocky water below. Beside the ruined bridge was a steep, twisty path down to where the water formed the pond that was our 'swimming hole'.

The fine, white silver-sand was almost as important to us as the water was. It sifted through our fingers like fine cornmeal. Sometimes, in early spring or late autumn when swimming was out of the question we went down, anyway, to play in the sand. Then it would be hard and crusty and cold to touch. But in summer it was still warm even long after the sun went down. During high summer, the sand burned our bare feet. We skimmed the surface at a run or else went very, very slowly grinding each foot down until it reached the cooler damp sand underneath. All of those summers in the sand are telescoped into one golden memory.

There were often gangs of children; sometimes it was only me and one or two of the other kids; occasionally it was just me, alone. I made houses and holes and pictures and sculptures. We jumped and stamped and rolled and buried each other for day after endless day. Once we all worked upon a giant person lying out in the middle of the pit like a sphinx; it was a perfect sculpture. Even us little kids did as we were bidden and shaped arms and fingers and toes or just brought more, damp sand to add to the huge structure. Then we joined in to stamp it to death at the end of the day.

Playing in the sand was the best way to get warm again if you were cold from swimming too much. Sometimes in late spring we would be fooled by the fine, white, dry layer of sand on the top into thinking it was time to go swimming.

Cum on. Let's go swimming.

Ain't time yet. School ain't out.

Yeah, but lookie here. This here sand is hot. Ma won't know.

She will.

Not if you don't tell her. Sissy- sissy pants.

OK but we won't get our swimmin'suits, OK?.

Down we clambered and over to the sunny shallows where in July the water was usually hot. One test with our bare toes soon saved us the bother of taking all our clothes off.

Judas Priest! I ain't goin' in that.

My first water adventures began there at the shallows where the bank was black and muddy, with a gradual deepening of the water as it sloped gently towards the middle; the place, in fact, where I caught the fish. It must have been where Tonie took me as a small baby; it is certainly where my memories begin.

I am little, really very young and I sit stripped in the warm water at the edge. Everybody else is far away and I am alone in my watery world. My legs have a strange yellow glow where the sun shines on them through the water. I make my legs change colour by carefully lifting then out and letting them sink in again. A dragonfly, blue and shiny, lands on my arm. I sit very, very still unafraid as its wings beat faster and faster to keep it from doing a nosedive. Then, as suddenly as it arrived, off it flew again. I begin to cry in loneliness. One of the big boys comes across to me. He carried me piggyback through the deep water, wading neck high until he couldn't touch bottom and then swimming with me on his back through the current to the other side. There on the far bank the water is deep even near the edge. He flings me up on the bank and goes back to join the others in their elaborate game of tag. They leap from tree to tree and the one who is 'it' must touch somebody else who then has to drop in the water and swim to the bank and get the next person. I can't join in. I play with some sticks for a little while but soon begin to cry again. I want to go back to my play place in the warm sunshine. I am floated back to the other side in the centre of a huge pink inner tube and left again to play with the pink, ballooned ring for company. I never remember Mama going swimming with us.

Halsie told me recently that one day I disappeared completely under the water and Benny jumped several feet from the diving board to pull my submerged, inert body out onto the mud bank where he hit my back until tears and water came shooting out as I coughed and spluttered alive again. Whilst Jiggy was small and fidgety, Benny was solid and sturdy.

About nine or ten feet from the shallow edge there was a large, submerged rock. It was wedge shaped and made a counter slope from that of the bank. It was like walking up hill in the water. On its far edge was a small seat like depression – a hollowed out chair. The swimming hole really was a hole and this rock marked the spot where it suddenly grew deep. I could sit on my rock throne, only waist high in the water but at the edge of deep water.

I began to swim gradually but I learned to swim suddenly. The shallow end was where I practiced, usually alone, getting first my feet and then my hands off the bottom. I spent a lot of time propelling myself around inside an inner tube. There were usually two or three of these at the swimming hole; they were community property. Two planks of wood held in place by boulders were fixed up for diving. One was on the nearside for shallow diving. Here the water was about six feet deep. The other was fixed into a tree at the far side where the water was always much deeper.

To test the depth at any given time, it fluctuated with the seasons and weather, one of the bigger kids would jump off the shallow board, holding his nose, and with his free hand extended above his head. We could calculate how deep the water was by how much hand stuck out above the water when he stood on the bottom. This test wasn't necessary for the high board; the water was always deep in the channel. I was not allowed anywhere near the high board. By the time I was old enough and big enough to consider jumping off, the swimming hole was depopulated by people going into the service or off to war work leaving just the younger kids to play about. When the high board rotted through it was not put back. But, from very early on I was a regular user of the low board. I would walk the length, holding an inner tube around my belly with one hand and my nose with the other and jump or drop off the end making a satisfying smack as the water hit the tube. This was a regular part of my ritual from the time I was about three.

Sometime during the summer before my fourth birthday, it was probably 4th of July when we always had a family picnic; almost all of the family were down at the swimming hole. They decided that Rinkie had to learn to swim. I ran squealing away but Carl captured me and carried me out to the end of the low diving board. Down below in the water all of my brothers, a sister or two and others from the neighbourhood had formed a ring. I clung to Carl who threw me in anyway. I held my nose and fell in like the lead sinker on a fishing line. I came up to see a circle of laughing faces. They played 'touch-me-not' as I frantically tried to reach one and then another. They always ducked out of reach as I dog paddled towards them, kicking up a frenzy. Until, giving up I made for the big rock and pulled myself up onto its familiar safety. Then they all yelled and cheered. "She's done it. Rinkie can swim". I was lifted high and carried home on somebody's back to tell Ma, "Rinkie can swim".

I practiced my new found skill determinedly and by the end of the summer was quite a competent swimmer. It was probably just the next summer when I could swim all the way across at the narrowest part unaided. However, I never really gave up playing with the inner tubes. They were so reassuringly big and such fun to try and sink since you couldn't no matter how hard you tried to.

It was just one or two years later when I was five or six and able to roam about on my own that I broke the family rule. I went down to the swimming hole alone. It was a sunny late spring or early summer morning, hot and still but not humid. We could go and play in the sand alone but it was forbidden to go in the water unless there was at least one other person there. I knew I was being naughty.

The water was brown, green and dancing yellow in the sunny places at the edge. I played about here at the shallow bits waiting in the hope that somebody else would come along. Nobody did. Then I dared myself to have a real swim and to go all the way across. I set out towards the dark, black-green water on the other side. That side was lined with trees, it was deep almost to the edge and the bottom was covered with slimy sticks and weeds. I didn't like to touch bottom there so I planned a quick turn around.

The water, at first warm and heavy, grew colder and more brisk as I reached the current where the brook ran into the pond. It was hard swimming across the current and, as I stopped to tread water and catch my breath, the head of a black snake appeared. It was coming towards me from in under the trees at the far side. It chased me, anyway I thought it did, and I turned tail in panic to swim back to the other side. I paddled as fast as I could but it seemed to be gaining on me. My legs wouldn't move fast enough as, overcome by panic, I willed them to go faster but they seemed to go slower and slower. I made it back to the other side and lay sick and sobbing in the warm mud near the edge. The snake had by this time lost any interest it may have had in me and was nowhere to be seen. Of course, since I was engaged in a forbidden act, swimming alone, I couldn't tell anybody about it. Like other forbidden actions later on, I kept the guilt and fear inside.

Swimming was not the only water activity. We had all kinds of delightful pastimes. One hot day Jimmy and I were playing at the shallow end. It was too hot to play in the sand and we were tired of swimming. We started a muck making game in the dark clay along the edge. It had a rotting, putrid smell but that didn't put us off. We danced about making holes in the soft clay with our feet. Gradually, by working our feet like pistons, we made ourselves each a hole to sit in, buried up to our waists in slimy black filth. We then started rubbing it all over each other's head, hair, face and all. We slurried mud on our arms, torso, neck and ears, by now we were wild with excitement and launched ourselves from the holes into a magnificent war dance.

Then, hand in hand, we went running into the water to wash clean again leaving long dark trails of black in the water as the mud washed away. We started all over again. We plastered ourselves black and went into our yelling singing dance like the savages we were. This time we lay in the sun to let it dry and had the idea to go home, just as we were, to get something to eat. Up across the sand pit we ran, along the black tarred road, hot and soft under our feet. We gained the dirt road and then the lane. Out of breath and panting, we suddenly slowed down at the corner of the house. We knew Mama wouldn't let us come in stinking of pond mud. We whispered plans of how to get in without Ma knowing. But she always knew everything. When we looked in the kitchen window, there she was as always. We waited about a bit, hiding in case she went up to the backhouse but she didn't. Flies buzzed. We could see the bread and jelly on the table. Subdued by the quietness, we abandoned the idea of stealing food and went all of the long way back to the swimming hole to wash. We didn't consider using the brook, which was nearer in case we got told off for making the water dirty. By the time we got back, having run lickity-split down the tarred road, the mud was beginning to tighten our skin and crack in places. We looked piebald. We started another dance in the sand pit, throwing handfuls of white sand up in the air and standing underneath the shower of crystals. Then, of a sudden, without consultation we went running down the hill' straight out and off the diving board into a frenzied arm thrashing war dance. We emerged as clean as ever we could be with only faint smears of black in out of the way places to show there had been a metamorphosis. We went home to eat.

What have you two been up to?

Nothin'

Chapter Twelve
November Day

Cocoa and toast was what I always had once the big kids had gone to school. Mama had tea. Today we sat in the kitchen – not out on the doorstep like on my birthday. 'Indian summer', Mama had said then.

The cranberry rolled away
Before Thanksgiving Day
Said she: they'll make a sauce of me,
If I should stay.

It was my latest song; a school song Tonie had taught to me.

The pumpkin rolled away
Before Thanksgiving Day
Said he: they'll make a pie of me,
If I should stay.

Mama smiled her secret smile. The kitchen was quiet except for the hiss of the kettle on the back of the range. No flies buzzed about. The flypaper hung, ignored, dried flies black on the amber sticky stuff – long ladybugs swinging in the warmth.

'Go down and collect the eggs, Rinkie, and we'll make pumpkin pies.'

I jumped up and put my feet into the first pair of shoes by the door and charged out to be stopped short by Mama's shout.

'Put on a coat'

She held out Jimmy's corduroy jacket ready for my arms. It was much too big but quicker than the new birthday snowsuit which could have gotten covered in chicken doos anyway. My hands stayed inside the sleeves but I pounded away out the door.

'And a hat', called me back.

I pushed my hands out and pulled on my own red woolly hat with the pompom and stomped back across the dooryard with heavy feet.

Tiny grains of snow hissed as they fell, salting the path leading down to the barns, outlining the track of footprints up to the house. It was the first really cold day. Yesterday's mud, frozen into small hills, made the too big shoes even harder to walk in. I tried to step in every one of the backward footprints. Each was double the size of mine so I had to play giant steps all the way.

The door of the chicken coop was stuck. I pushed hard and fell in as it suddenly gave way, sending chickens squawking in all directions. Some flew up to the roosts and others round and round. Johnny had already fed them and they soon settled. A few scratched for corn in the sawdust but mostly they sat and watched. Finding eggs was easy in the winter. I knew where to look – my hand slipped easily under warm bodies in the nesting boxes that lined the long side of the coop underneath the eves of the sloping roof. These eggs were warm and smooth in my fingers. Others were in empty boxes under the matted hay and already cool. One lay in the corner on the floor covered in droppings. I wiped it on my sleeve.

'Only seven today – no, eight, nine.

I counted as I put them carefully into the little wooden berry box – red with summer strawberry juice. It was a bit broken, but I held it carefully, tight against my belly as I backed out of the door and shooed the hen, which was trying to escape, inside again.

'It's too cold out here. You'll freeze your gizzard off.

The turkey ran away
Before Thanksgiving Day
Said he: They're sure to roast me
If I should stay.

You're not running away; we need your eggs.
Pumpkin pie needs lots of eggs.'

Going back up to the house was quicker if you didn't try to keep to the footsteps. I put my hat over the box to keep the eggs from rolling away and sidestepped up the slippery hill. The snow had stopped. There wasn't even enough to make proper footprints. It was just salt and pepper snow. But it was cold and I puffed out steam in long streamers.

There was smoke pouring out of the chimney as it sent sparks up into the snow dark sky.

Mama was waiting with the pumpkin already stewing and the molasses tin on the table. Her arms were covered in flour as she wiped white hands down her front. She carefully lifted the hat to look at the eggs.

'Those hens are sure lazy today, Mama. They only gave us nine.'

'Nine is enough, more than enough. Get your things off and stand by the stove. I'll make you more cocoa in a minute.'

> *The celery stalked away*
> *Before Thanksgiving Day*
> *Said he: they're sure to crunch me*
> *If I should stay.*

'What's celery?'

'A vegetable. We can't grow it here; it's too cold. '

'But we've got a fire. Can't you smell it? It's making sparks up the chimney.'

'Sparks up the chimney!'

Mama sprang into action. She ran out into the dooryard and ran back in again. Mama never ran; I'd never seen her run. I was too scared to move but I heard her on the phone.

'Send the fire engine. The chimney's on fire. Send somebody, quick.'

We went out and stood together in the dooryard looking up at the sparks landing on the roof. I held her hand. We could hear the fire siren. People began to arrive and stood on the hill around about the house. The fire engine came up the driveway. Lots of men came running. My brother Carl came too.

Mama and I went inside again. She didn't ever go out much, not by herself, just sometimes to Mrs.MacArthur's where we got our water from her pump. The firemen had to go to the brook to fill their tank. Then they hosed the roof with great spurts of water. I saw them through the window.

'I'm cold Mama'

'We'll put on your snowsuit'

Once I was pulled into my red snowsuit I thought we'd go out.

OK. *Can we go to Mrs. MacArthur's now?*

'We'll see.'

But she didn't put on her coat and we stayed in the kitchen.

'Can I go out on the hill?'

'We'll see.'

That usually meant 'yes' but today it meant 'no'. She stayed in the kitchen and I looked out the window at the people crowded on the hill pointing and talking.

Two men came in the door and went upstairs to see if the roof was burning inside. I followed but they were down again before I got to the top. One picked me up and took me back down to the bottom. By then Mama was standing in the other room – the room off the kitchen which also had a stove – a pot bellied Franklin Stove with a long stove pipe. The one we sat around in winter and told stories and cracked hickory nuts. It had only just been put up for the winter. Its fire was out now. It oozed water and had a crack nearly all around the lower rim. It was still steaming. A great pool of rusty water spread on the floor around the stove.

'Can we go to Mrs. MacArthurs's now?'

'No'

'Can we make the pumpkin pies?'

'We'll see'

I knew we wouldn't, not with all those people standing on the hill looking.

Carl didn't go back to work right away; he made us soup on the oil burner which we usually only used in the summer.

Mama didn't cry until Pop came home. He was really mad about the water on the floor and the crack in the stove.

'God dam sons of bitches didn't know their asses from their elbows. You don't pour water on a hot stove'

It still worked, though. We had a fire that night to dry up the water. But always afterwards the potbelly grew red hot just where the crack was. Jimmy and Halsie said it would melt if it got red all the way around. But it never did.

Chapter Thirteen

Paint

Whenever we were asked what we had been doing our standard reply was,

Nothin'. We ain't been doin' nothin' much.

Nothing much is what we always did. In the village, down behind Honon's store was the town dump. It was another of our playgrounds.

Hey... lookie 'ere...see what I found.

What?

Cans and cans of the stuff; Com'ere.

Jeese - look at it all. It must have been Old Man Upham's. Are they full?

Naw.. but look there's some in all of 'em.

Yeah .. white, black , red , green. It must've been when they painted the factory... we'll do the barn.

We'll do the barn and the chicken coop with this... and the kitchen stove.

Naw.. Ma's got special stuff for the stove.

How we gonna get it home? Don't tell the others. It'll be ours... we'll surprise them. Can you carry it?

Naw...

Without another word we tore off at a run - seemingly wound up by the same elastic band - took the shortcut down the railroad tracks, up the bank of the cutting and into the barn by the back way. We quickly found the cart and rattled our way back again taking turns riding and being pulled. The cart couldn't run across ties so the tracks were out. We tore down the dirt road past the house without even looking. Once onto the main road, bare feet slapping the hot tar, we made good time and both coasted down the hills. On the way past Danny's house we shouted for him to join us.

We slowed to a walk and pulled the empty cart in turns, went across the tracks at the crossing and took the long way in behind the feed store, past the lumber yard road and into the dump. The paint cans were just as we'd left them. We loaded up and meandered our way home again.

We'll do the barn the chicken coop and the upstairs.

Yeah - nobody but us goes up there.

Don't tell Pop or Carl. We can tell Halcy. It'll be a surprise for Ma. Ya wanna help us, Danny? It'll be fun.

The plan to paint the barn or even the chicken coop became submerged into the grand order of things. We would start with the whole upstairs - the place where all of the boys used to sleep. Now the war was on and the big boys were in the Navy; nobody went up there much except us little kids on rainy days. The older girls were married and away from home that meant everybody left at home could sleep downstairs.

Like the rest of the house this upstairs room was never finished. It ran the whole length and breadth of the building without even uprights to mark off where the separate rooms were supposed to be. It soared away up to the rafters like a church. Another story was to have been inserted but that was one of Pop's pipe dreams. The room was only half floored; they had run out of boards; somebody said they had used the boards in the stove to keep warm in the winter of 1928/29. The place where I had fallen through was still visible beside the landing. On the floored area all across the front of the house were the line of iron bedsteads. The tea chest flooring on the back would bear the weight of a cat but children had to balance on the narrow 2x4's to get across. I knew this from experience having once taken the quick way down. Since then I was always careful to stick to the middle of the door gangway unless, it was for a dare or I had other reason to go across the hard way.

Except for the beds, the rest of the place was a repository for the unused or unwanted. Various chests, trunks, boxes, broken furniture and the like were carefully balanced on the 2x4's or else perched on the precious floored surface under or behind the beds. In summer the pot-bellied stove from the "living room" was dismantled and put up here to make more room downstairs. It looked like a fat old man sleeping beside his stovepipe hat. I often played beside it and with it in my more solitary moments. There was also a redundant kitchen range up there - I don't know why- since the one in the kitchen was in use winter and summer in those days. Later we got a couple of oil stoves for using in the hot, hot summers; but nobody ever took the kitchen stove apart to store it upstairs. The Pot-bellied one went up there every June and came down again in the fall.

Anyway - the plan was to paint the upstairs - it had never been done. By the time we got home with the cart we had already made a long detour to the swimming hole and gone in, bare assed, to cool off. Somebody had come along and sent us home to get trunks- so we went back up the hot tarred road to the lane and then took the cart up the driveway carefully and parked it next to one of the rusting cars.

Pop can't know. Don't tell nobody - see!

He will know even if we don't tell him. He'll find out about it. He'll SEE it when he comes home.

He ain't gonna. We'll move it - see.

If Pop, or Carl, found out about our plans or even saw the paint we had no chance. Being the only girl, I was sent in to find out where everybody was and to create a distraction. Ma was in the kitchen, as always, having a "set down" and a cup of tea. Pop was nowhere about. I asked for bread and peanut butter and jelly for all of us. Mama got up to get it and the boys streaked away past and up the stairs lugging the cans of paint. They had to make two trips. We were safe. Mama never went upstairs nowadays.

We stuffed in the thick bread Ma had thinly spread with peanut butter and jelly, gulped down the warm, nearly sour milk whilst standing at the table or dancing about the kitchen on one leg. We flung our shorts at the door and retrieved our suits from the stonewall fence outback where they were always put to dry. They were now dry but stiff. We pulled them open, stepping into them as we ran back down to the swimming hole. The plan to paint the chicken coop, the barn and the upstairs temporarily abandoned, we joined most of the rest of the kids from Hawleyville at the swimming hole. It was summer hot and time to perfect diving, jumping, splashing and swimming from the big rock to the side and back again, trying not to put your feet down into the tangled sticks and weeds on the bottom. But that day was the start of it - finding the paint and getting it upstairs without anybody knowing.

Summer rainy days were not too common but it only took one to get us started. Upstairs the rain hammered the roof, trapped the hot air into a protective canopy and muffled our squeals and shouts. Jimmy and I got tired of doing head-over-heels, ass-over-teakettle, on the beds or jumping from one to the other all down the line, corks popping from Pop's home brewed hard cider. Tickling each other had made us too tired to laugh anymore. Exhausted, we lay on our backs looking up at the rafters and listened to the rain.

We could see the little white chalk circles drawn on the undersides of the roof boards and away high, high on the roof struts and rafters.

How did they do it? They must have been monkeys once. Jiggy said I'm one. They must'uv used to be monkeys.
Stupid!! They climbed up the posts, swung out along the struts and put their mark - see some of 'em are round and some oval. Lookie - that one - way out there....

I looked and knew I couldn't add to them. Neither could Jimmy. We were too damn little. Even standing on the end of the highest bed we could get nowhere near the lowest strut. It must have been when all the big boys were home that they started to make their marks on the rafters. Who could make the highest one? That was the contest. We couldn't play that for sure. It was then we thought of the paint.

Right ..... let's.....

We started on the pot-bellied stove right away. I'm not sure when or where we got the paintbrushes but we had them. It could be that our paint cans from the dump were added to some already up there. We worked hard and soundlessly painting the black, somewhat rusting stove, white. It was harder than it looked to get the paint to cover the surface. It slipped and slithered off making dribbles down the legs and you no sooner got one part covered than it ran off again. It was a bit like trying to put frosting on a hot cake.

O.K. That's it.

It looks good don't it?

It ain't done yet. We gotta leave it to dry. It needs another coat.

We stuck the brushes in one of the now nearly empty cans of white, wiped ourselves off pretty good and went out into the brightly washed day. The rain had stopped. Mama called after us from the kitchen door. "What have you been up to? Where you going now?"

Nothin'

We're goin down to the brook, OK?

Jimmy got some kerosene from the barrel and we wiped off what paint we could from our legs and faces. We took off down the hill to the brook before anybody could spot us and ask what we were doing. We knew where there was a piece of soap hidden down there when somebody wanted to wash and we scrubbed with that and sandy gravel from the bank.

It didn't rain for a while after that but we took to going upstairs anyway when we had nothing else to do. We got better and better at painting and hardly got it on ourselves at all. I can't remember the sequence of colors but most of the paint was white so I guess we gave it another coat or two of that. The brushes were stiff as sticks by now but we found some more. When we started on the colors, I became one with the mixing and merging paint - the subtle colours of white mixed with red and green, soot streaked and thick, transformed the stove into a living creature. I don't know which came first - finding a whole small can of bright blue or putting on the initial coat. I do know the blue paint was another dump find and it added the final touch.

We were true artists at work; my first realization of the process that has not yet given me up. We had just a little red and green. We made spots and splurges and stripes in a changing pattern of shapes and colors - we painted the inside of the lid even though it was covered in soot and blackened the paint. We also painted the inside of the fire door. But it was the blue that finished it off. The blue stripes against the white stood out like a flag.

How many hours, days, and weeks we worked on our art is lost in the endlessness of childhood. Who knows? We didn't. We didn't even care.

As suddenly as it was started - it was finished.

That's OK. No more anymore, OK?

Yeah OK It's Ok in't it?

Pretty good.

PRETTY GOOD!

From then on we found other things to do and forgot all about the painting plans for the barn and chicken coop.

Pretty soon it was almost time for school again. Our new shoes arrived from the Sears Roebuck catalogue. Our bare feet had been drawn around weeks ago and the pattern sent off with the order. We tried them on. Both Jimmy and me had new shoes that year. Pop must have been making enough or, maybe, the big boys sent money from the Navy.

How Pop decided when to go and get the stove set up for the winter we never knew. One day we would come home from school and there it would be, alight. We mostly ignored the weather and signs of winter coming. The kitchen was always warm with a wood fire going in the black stove there. We needed it for cooking.

One day we came in from school to hear Pop shouting and stomping about upstairs.

"Those God Damned kids. Judas Priest! What in the hell; who in the

hell did this? Judas H. Priest. You God damn KIDSSS Come here."
We belted off to hide as Pop came staggering down the stairs carrying
the stovepipes all covered in white paint with coloured splashes.

"You God Damned Kids"

Carl, who had come home early to help him down with the stove couldn't hide the grin beneath his stern look and we knew we'd be OK. We came back again. I went and hid behind Mama. She said nothing at all but just stood and watched. They carried our flagship down the stairs and out the kitchen door to the yard. I still thought it looked pretty good. Jimmy was white beneath his freckles. They put the pieces of stovepipe, including the elbow bend, which we had forgotten to paint, beside the stove like two arms sticking up and one foot sticking out. It was something like a snowman with no scarf but painted on clothes.

"You God Damned Kids. When the hell did you do this? It MUST have been you two! Judas Priest!"
"Can't you leave anything to hell alone?"
Pop got a can, filled it with kerosene, poured it over the stove and lit a

match.

"Get the HELL out of the way. Get the hell out of here!"

The flames leaped into the air in a blue torch before settling down to lick the top and sides of the stove which now burned brighter and hotter on the outside than it ever did on the inside. Our beautiful colours burned red and blue and green and orange with a pillar of black smoke rising up in the air higher than the house.

Pop danced around the burning furnace, an Indian in a War Dance - whooping and hollering - jumping and stamping his feet in frenzied oscillations, stealing our wickedness for himself. We watched quietly and began to know the truth of the family story that he had burned his own house down by playing with matches when a mere toddler. He loved fire.

It burned for a long time - he kept adding more kerosene -then made a fire of kindling inside the belly. It burned long after we had been sent to bed.

In the morning, there it stood in the dooryard, a blackened rusty accusing pitiful thing. Rusty stains streaked the blackened belly. Drips of thickened paint still oozed down the legs. There were rusty holes in the stovepipe. Pop was nowhere to be seen.

Mama sent us off to school- our not quite new shoes scuffed along the fallen leaves.

Judas Priest.

God dammed fool.

Judas Priest the God dammed fool. Judas Priest the God damned fool. The God DAMNED FOOL, *God Damned Fool, God damned fool god damned fool god damned fool.......Judas Priest* THE GOD DAMNED FOOL.

Go to hell you God damned fool.

That afternoon the stove was still in the yard. Mama was on her knees in front of it. Two new stovepipes stood nearby. The old ones lay on their side by the fence where they were to stay for years. Carl had been back to help her put on the special stove blacking. It was now all black and shiny new. We helped buff it up with newspaper. It looked BETTER than new.

In the morning there was a funny smell when we got up. The first fire of the winter was making the potbelly glow red.

POP grinned from behind his newspaper, "You know if it gets red ALL the way around it MELTS". It seems that it was not just a claim made by the boys. It would melt. Pop confirmed it. He leered at us and took another puff on his pipe.

Better than new

Chapter Fourteen

Going to the Store

Even before I went to school Mama might sometimes send me to the store on my own. She would write out a list and send me off.

I knew the way, down the drive way, out past Mrs.MacArthurs, onto the tarred road , down past the Gilberts, on down the hill over the bridge, past the 'old store' on the corner where the 'Van's' now lived , along a bit and over the railroad crossing and there was Honon's store. It had two 'lollypop' gas pumps in the front and a long porch

As often as not Skippy, the dog followed me. He usually went where I did. This day he ran barking down the hill across the road in front of a car that had to brake with a screech. The man inside, I didn't know his name but he knew me, leaned out and gave me hell for not keeping the dog 'under control'. Later Pop gave me hell too but couldn't keep his eyes from laughing as he said, 'Don't swear at people.' Apparently I had stood with my hands on my hips, stamped my foot and shouted 'Well, what in the hell do you expect ME to do about it? I didn't tell him to come'; words no doubt that had been said by big brothers when I tagged along with them and got into trouble.

The Store had a screen door in from the porch and just beside it on the right as you entered was the Post Office with a high counter and a window. Beside the window was a tier of gleaming wooden boxes with black numbers and a glass window on each one. That is where we got our mail, from Box number 25. You knew not to ask if the box was empty.

To the left beside the door were all kinds of things. The dreaded long, dark stockings, which wouldn't stay up even with elastic garters, sat beside the workman's gloves, sewing thread, elastic, boots, overalls and other things I now know as 'Haberdashery'. You could get almost everything at Honon's.

It was quite a big room and shelved all around from floor to ceiling. At the far end opposite the door and sitting a few feet out into the room was a counter piled high with all sorts of foodstuff. The bit in the middle was clear and this is where Mr. Honon stood to serve. I would shyly go up to the counter, stand up on tiptoe and produce my list along side a penny.

'Mama said put it on the bill and I can have a penny candy'.

He would set to filling the order, never very much maybe a can of soup and some crackers and cheese. The shelves were pilled high with dry goods and he had a long pole with a kind of grabber on the end to reach the high stuff.

He wore a long light brown coat with pockets in winter and sheet sleeves with some kind of bands to hold them up in summer. One of his arms was smaller and shiny and didn't bend like the other one.

As well as being our grocer he was an undertaker in Newtown. (I was to see him in his black suit, in the big funeral parlour in Newtown not too many years later when he buried first Mama and then four years later Pop.) His withered arm was, so it was told, because he had caught 'blood poisoning' from one of the dead bodies.

I liked watching him cut off the cheese from the big round under a glass dome that stood on the counter next to where he served. He had a strange contraption for serving the cheese. I thought it might be because his hand didn't work. The glass lid had a cord in the top that went up through a pulley in the ceiling with a weight attached to the other end so it stayed out of his way and he could use both hands to chop the cheese with the wide knife that sat under the glass beside the cheese round. He then lifted the cheese on the flat part of the knife onto some waxed paper that he carefully folded and put in a brown paper bag. Then he gave a little tug on the rope and the lid came back down to cover the cheese.

Just beside the counter was a long glass case with sliding doors. It was full of boxes and boxes of penny candy and Tootsie Rolls™ and bars of chocolate and Mama's favourite Necco™ wafers; that cost about a nickel. You could get quite a few things for a penny and Mr. Honon would put them into a little bag. I could take a long time choosing and sometimes he would hurry me along by selecting them himself and giving me one extra.

Mr Honon put most of our goods 'on the bill'. In fact if it were not for him I am sure we would often have gone hungry. That 'bill' was not paid in full until long after most of us kids had left Hawleyville. Indeed, not until Pop died I think. I believe they paid what they could when they could. Once Mama had some money, it may have been from one of the boys who had left home during the war. It was $100 dollars and she sent me secretly down to the store with it in an envelope tied into a small cloth bag. I was not to tell anybody not even Pop. I was to be VERY CAREFUL not to stop and dawdle and not to lose it. When I gave it to Mr. Honon, his face went red and he smiled at me like he never had done. It was spring, long past Christmas, but on the counter was a basket full of gingerbread men with stuck on Santa faces. He put three in a bag and asked me to choose some candy for the penny Mama had given me; he gave me lots and lots. I thought Christmas had come back again.

Of course not all of our food could be grown,shot or foraged. I remember a meat man that came one day a week. Mama would go out to the road to choose something. She could not put that 'on the bill' so I suppose she got what she had money for. Tonie said he swore a lot and mama called him "too-mucha- discustin".

Mr Honon did not keep fresh meat but he had lots of other things. Bacon, salt pork, cured beef, cold cuts, and cans of corn beef, Spam and other cans and packages of things Mama would put with what ever she had to make a meal. We almost always had potatoes and other root vegetables. We had our own supply of eggs from the hens and then later from Carl at the farm. Salt pork and beans made with molasses and canned tomatoes Pop liked but I didn't. One of my favourite suppers was Shredded Wheat covered with just enough boiling water to stop it being crunchy and covered with salt, pepper and smothered with butter.

Mama made many meals based on eggs. Pancakes with butter and maple syrup from our own bottled stock could not be bettered. Eggs boiled, fried, scrambled or made into soup were the basis of many a quick supper. Eggs soup was made by breaking the eggs into a bowl, adding pieces of bread and pouring boiling water on top and quickly mixing it up with a fork. I think she sometimes added eggs to chicken broth to make it go further. We had 'French toast', bread pudding with cinnamon and raisins and Pop's favourite 'eggnog' with nutmeg sprinkled on the top. Best of all was ice cream made in the hand freezer using ice from the ice man or else from an early winter freeze.

If times were good we might get broken cookies from a tin at Honon's and rarely oranges or other fruit. We almost always had apples.

When winter came and Jimmy and I walked to school we always stopped at the store to get warm. I think there had been a stove in the middle behind the post office partition but I remember best the hot air radiator that was installed when a furnace was put in the basement. We would go in shivering and stand on the radiator and let the warm air heat us from our frozen feet to the tips of our noses. One cold, snowy day Mr. Honon asked us to show him our hands. I held mine out fearfully in case I had done something wrong. He looked carefully and went to the rack beside the door and selected two pairs of brown work gloves one for Jimmy and one for me. Mine were much too big but they were warm and I danced my way to school wriggling my fingers all the way. I don't suppose he put those on the bill. He was essentially very kind to us and we knew it even if we did call him 'Old man Honon' behind his back.

Chapter Fifteen

Hunting Food

If I shut my eyes I can still see them, hanging in great black clumps almost too high to reach. Protected by briers and always the last to come, blackberries ended the berry season that had begun in high summer. The early morning dew was already cold on my bare feet as I went down behind the barn to pick them. I felt sorry for Peter Rabbit anew as I ate my blackberry and milk breakfast, rubbing at the long scratches on my arms that were the penalty you had to pay for the pleasure of purple milk. Poor Peter who was a bad little bunny only had camomile tea; I had as many blackberries as I could pick.

All the Rockies in the Dell

They all know but they won't tell

That was our motto. We were a tribe and had tribal rituals. We could count off the year by what we could pick when. In early spring we foraged for dandelion greens. We had kitchen knives to poke into the soft earth down beside the long root. Then you had to pull so hard you probably fell over backward and spilled the whole colander full. *Not like that. Don't cut off the leaves first or it'll fall apart.*

Loosen it up and then pull it all out. Ma'll take off the leaves. Don't take that one. It'll be too bitter. Never take the ones with flowers.

I didn't like dandelion greens much; Pop loved them. But I did like the flowers. Ma did too. She always put my bunch in the jelly glass full of water in the middle of the table. They only lasted a day once you picked them. In the grass they stayed yellow longer and then turned into fluffy clock heads to blow and wish on. Ma liked them as much as her mess of greens. I was sure of that.

To get more dandelions, we often went across the road into the pasture where Bill Bakey kept his cows. In the early summer the cow flops were green and squashy and to be avoided. But later on, when the dandelions were too bitter to cook, the sun baked them into hard and crusty pats. By then we were on the look out for strawberries. There were lots of places where wild strawberries grew.

Our tribe went far afield secretly locating the places where the closely grouped green leaves with the small white flowers promised strawberry jam. We would set out in the morning and walk the boundaries to check on the progress of our patches. Tonie always knew where the best ones would be. We went secretly and stealthily.

Don't tell anybody else. Don't tell the Van's. See, they've got little white berries, lots of them. We'll get lots.

Then one day it would be the right day. Sunny and bright we set off with pans and baskets. We had to be careful not to pull out the plants but to only take the ripe berries.

You can leave on the hulls but you must never, never pull up the whole plant.

Why?

Because, that's why!

But why not?

'cause they're not like dandelions, you don't eat the greens. You just eat the berries. Ya' don't eat the hulls.

Ma takes off the hulls. If you pull up the plants we won't have any next year. That's why not. If you take off the hulls now they get too squashed; so pick the berry and the hull.

OK

One year something went wrong with the strawberry plan. It should have been a bumper year. Tonie had promised that we would get lots and lots. The whole gang of us, me, Jimmy, Hal, Billy and Tonie set off to walk up the old road to where she knew there was a whole field full of fruit. On the way we met the Van's coming back. They were carrying two washtubs full of strawberries; stems, leaves plants and berries piled high together. They had raided Tonie's field. They had ruined the biggest patch in the village. Tonie never forgave them and it still rankles her over half a century later. That year we had to make do with lesser pickings.

Lots of other kinds of berries grew around about. Blueberries grew in the fields on the hill beside the upper road to school. Somebody big always had to go too. They grew on low bushes and were hard to pick. It took a long time to get enough for pie. They turned your lips a nice blue colour. Elderberries were not much fun because they didn't taste good right away. They had to be made into jelly. They grew too high from the ground for me to reach. I didn't bother much with them; the same for red and black currants, too sour. We didn't have many raspberries growing nearby. It was strawberries that were my joy.

We had apple trees and a plum tree and Mrs. Turril had a pear tree and another apple tree. She always let us come and pick up the windfalls. The plum tree was my own special tree. It didn't grow many plums but it was just the right size to climb and had a 'Y' shaped seat formed by the lower branch. It was my dreaming tree and it told me the seasons by its pink flowers, green plums turned to yellow then purple. Birds sang their secrets to it and the tree told me.

Blackberries came in the fall after school had started again. We had plenty in our own land so we could pick them whenever we wanted. Even Mama would go and gather enough for a pie.

After blackberries came hickory nuts. We had to go further a field to find them and they did not have the instant reward of berries. Tonie and I would take a pail and go out on an autumn sunny day into the woods to collect nuts. They then had to dry off and be stored for a winter's evening when with a hammer and a flat iron on your lap you could crack nuts and make as much noise as you wanted while sitting around the stove in the other room. Three kids with three hammers and three flat irons could make a wonderful anvil chorus. It took hours to get even a cupful of nutmeats; hickory nuts are so small and the meats so hard to get out. But we had winter hours to spare. The shells made a merry blaze in the stove. If we were lucky Carl made hickory nut fudge. He was the fudge expert just like he was the 'sugaring off' expert.

In looking for hickory nuts we were in direct competition with the squirrels. I often went on my own spying for nuts. There was a place down in front of Mrs. MacArthur's with a flat stone in the middle of a small triangle of land belonging to nobody. This was where the big kids waited for the High School bus and where the Sunday school bus picked us up. I might sit there on my own counting the nuts. We heaped the leaves in a big pile here and then ran and jumped into them like the savages we were. Or I would go kicking along the road in a coloured sea. The only sea I'd ever seen by then. I became for a time one of those leaves, detached from my tree but nevertheless going someplace. Burned into my eyes are the reds and gold, all mixed with bright sunshine, cold frost and the smell of damp, rotting undergrowth as I turned into the woods where last year's leaves were covered by a new carpet of yellow, brown, red and golden orange.

I went kicking along, not looking and ran into a tree. Underneath my feet was a hole and inside a very still squirrel with a nut in his mouth. His eyes watched me. Then he was up and away up the tree so quickly I fell over. Inside the tree I could see a store of nuts. Some were half eaten; others lay under the rotting last year's leaves. I grabbed handfuls and took them home in my pulled up coat.

Mama. Look. I found lots of nuts. Lookie.
Those are squirrels nuts; we can't eat them. We only save new nuts.
I'll take them back.

But I didn't. I used to go hunting squirrels with the boys even when I was just four or five. Pop let them take shotguns; sometimes he went too. There were rules about guns. Nobody was ever to point a gun at anybody; even if we were sure it wasn't loaded. You had to carry a gun with the barrel pointed down unless you were shooting at game.

Us little kids could only ever shoot a gun at a tin can target and then only if somebody helped us. But we liked going hunting and we could carry the bullets. These were round, red cylinders; they were very heavy.

You kids keep behind. Don't ever walk in front of the gun. KEEP QUIET! We're Indians, OK?

So off we went, single file in the woods, Hal, Billy, Jimmy and me. Maybe even Jiggy too. We might bag one or two squirrels. Our plans were always bigger that our result. Pop was the serious hunter. He went off on his own and he could come home with a dozen squirrels. He then set about skinning them. I don't know what happened to the skins. But the squirrels were for eating. He'd lay them out on the table in two neat rows of red. Their little legs stretched behind and in front with the heads gone. The squirrels had become meat and Pop was searching with a jack- knife to prise out the single shots embedded in their flesh. Mama rolled them in flour and fried them in bacon fat before she made them into a very bony stew. There were always one or two small black buckshot to be spit out. Without their skin and their long tails they didn't seem at all like my squirrel in the hollowed out tree. I think sometimes the older boys went hunting rabbits but I wasn't in on that.

Chapter Sixteen
Cowshit and Strawberries

In the two years after Jimmy started school 1937/1938, before I was old enough to go, I spent long hours on my own everyday. My favourite place to sit was my plum tree. Pop called it my crow's nest and used to ask me if I'd spied land yet. I didn't know what he meant until I read 'Treasure Island' some years later. But I did spy out the land. I could see over into the field behind Mrs. MacArthur's and one bright day I began to wonder what treasures I might find there. I was always on the look out for wild flowers. It was just past spring, the blossom on the plum tree had turned to little green lumps and the grass was long and still green.

Down the lane I ran with Skippy our black dog following. He always followed me. We whipped our way through the grass scaring grasshoppers and butterflies into flight. I'm sure I must have pulled up armfuls of some kind of blossom; I was always bringing something home. We reached the stonewall on the opposite corner and it was then I saw them. Under the bushes growing near the wall in telltale groups of three were the biggest strawberry leaves I had ever seen, a whole patch of them. Nestled in amongst the leaves were green and white blossoms and some already formed green berries; these too were bigger that normal. Usually strawberry plants were small and grew close to the ground in scattered patches. It was promised treasure trove on an undreamed of scale.

I started off home on the run with Skippy barking circles around me to tell Mama about my find. But by the time I got to the lane the boys had come home from school and I wasn't going to tell them. That was the beginning of the secret.

I took to visiting my strawberry patch nearly every day. Green buds opened into white flowers, white flowers into green fruit, green fruit into white, then pink and finally the full red of wild strawberries. Gradually nearly all of the flowers turned to green, then white, then pink berries; other more ordinary strawberries ripened and we went on our usual forages. But these took a long time. Then one day it rained and I didn't go.

It was hot afternoon the next day before Skippy and I took the by now well-marked trail to the far wall of Mrs. MacArthusr's lot. Even before I reached it I could see the red berries shining in the sun. That first day there were only a few ripe. I was going to take some home but they tasted so good hot off the plants and there were thousands more to come. I can't remember how many days I went to pick a few berries but I must have missed a day or two because one morning when Skippy and I arrived the plants were dripping with red berries.

Skippy went off to bark at a black box turtle; I sat on the ground picking strawberries. There were hundreds. Mine all mine. I ate them almost as fast as I could pick them. I crammed in three or four berries at a time and let the juice spurt onto my chin and drip down my bare chest. That must have been what gave me the idea.

I was going to take some home and made a little pile of them on a maple leaf but they kept falling off. So I ate more and more until I was stuffed with them. Still there were berries on the stems. I loved the colour where the juice stained my fingers. I rubbed berries in my hair and down my arms, squishing them in my fists until the juice

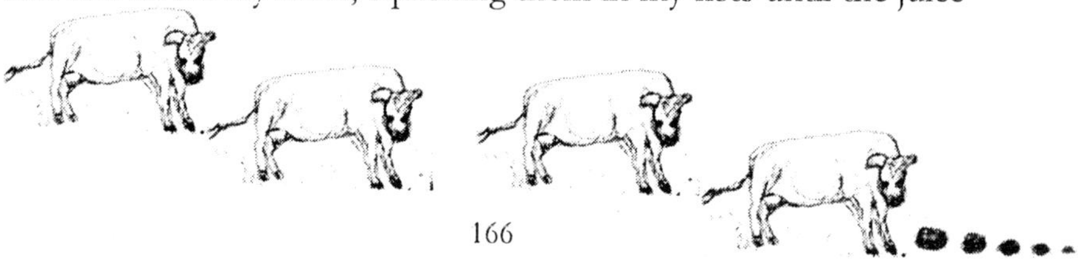

dripped in streams through my fingers in red rivers. I danced a war dance on the pile of berries at my feet and watched the juice bubble up through my toes. I hooted and hollered and slithered myself with strawberries until I had used every last berry in a mad frenzy.

What's black and white and red all over? Me. Me. Me.

Nobody's getting any. Mine all mine.

I lay on my back in the grass looking up at the sky with red arms and legs dancing in the air. Skippy, by now all barked out, came and licked my face. We decided to go home. We took the long way along the path the cows took through into the other field. The sun was hot. It had baked the cow flops into nice crusty pies. This was another of my favourite occupations on hot summer days; to seek a nice round crusty cow flop and stand in it with my bare feet to let the earthy green squeeze up between my toes. Now on this day when I was going home with my red feet and strawberry legs, I found a really lovely cow flop, just right; it was all crusty on top and hot with the sun.

My feet crunched through the warm crust into the juicy green filling. It bubbled up through my strawberry toes and mingled with the red juice; a delicious colour combination that I still love and use. I stepped in every cow flop along the way and arrived at the kitchen door streaked in slimy green and red.

Ma! Ma look at me!

Where have you been? Look at you! Go down and wash in the brook. You can't come in here like that.

But her eyes gave her away. That night Pop wanted to know if I'd saved him any strawberries and…

Who the hell smells of cow shit in here?

17 Chapter Seventeen

At Home With Mama

Watching the strawberries grow was only one of my adventures in the years at home alone with Mama when all the other children were at school or had left.

I loved to play in the brook. I would go down the steep steps at the front of the house along the dirt road and enter the shallow water where it came near the road just before the bridge. In fact, the same place where I washed off the strawberry juice and muck. It was where we all went to wash in summer and the soap was there underneath a stone.

I squat on the edge and watch the water. It was a good place to catch minnows but I have forgotten to bring a jam jar or one of the maple sap buckets. My hands mimic the movement of the water.

The brook is cool as it comes along out of the trees to bend in a slow curve into the sun. Long shapes dance under the willow branches, which trail their fingers in the water - reaching and reaching out of darkness to catch the sun as it slips past on the backs of minnows. It tumbles down a few rocks and is caught in a sandy trap. The banks are steeper here. The water flows more deeply and slower, forming a basin of sun and sand.

I stay as still as still and watch the water. A dragon flies by flashing his iris blue wings. Water bugs with tractor tires for feet carve the surface to and fro and below, their shadow selves make furrows in the sand.

Beyond the sand, where the water runs faster again, stones form a channel of light and color. Pebbles pink, white, ochre, brown, green, yellow, black and Indian red blow bubbles, shift their positions and ask to play.

In I step, bare feet churn sandy fields and send the water farmers scuttling away. An unknown time passes. Rinkie becomes one with the quiet and the water. Minnows scatter and the sun seeks out, first her reddened gold head, then each stone she has so carefully selected and put up on the grassy bank.

.......10...11...12...13 She counts her treasure. Quite suddenly she jumps up, puts them into her discarded pants and tramps naked up the lane, up the hill, up the path to the back door and home to Mama.

"Look. Look at my jewels". Mama admires the shiny gems and gives her an old crock to keep them safe. She puts them in one by one examining each treasure as it clunks to the bottom. She leaves them in the jar on the doorstep, gets clean pants and is off to play on the swing. When next she looks at them, the sun no longer glints or sparkles on their surface, the gleam is gone. Her shiny rocks are only dull ordinary common garden stones, lusterless. She dumps them out and kicks the container, which breaks into smithereens as it falls down the steps. Then the spell was broken. I was in the world again.

When I got tired of being by myself I would go and find Mama. She was usually in the kitchen but sometimes, if it was a nice day and the boys had brought up enough water, she would be working at the wash tub outside on the bench under the kitchen window. Her hands in soapy water resting on the scrubbing board with the piece of yellow soap resting on the little shelf above the crossway ribs, she'd stop and look with her usual smile. She might send me down to the brook for a small pail full of clean water for rinsing. There was always lots of washing to do. Even in winter when it wasn't much fun and the clothes stood up like ghosts on the line.

I liked giving Mama a rest. I stood up on a wooden box with my hands in the suds washing socks and other small things – like pants and vest and b.v.d.'s. I still don't know what bvd means but they were underclothes with a trap door at the back to allow you to 'do your business'. They were for men and boys. I had long bloomers that had elastic just above your knees made of flannelette in winter and panties in the summer. Panties were easier to wash.

Than Mama would twist the clothes to get the water out and rinse them once in cleaner water that got less clean as the morning went on. That was when she might send me down for some more. I would stand at the other end of the bigger things and twist the other way from her, a job I had long done with one of the boys or Tonie, then out back to the line to hang them up – me handing clothes pins, hanging the socks and other small things. Then together we would push up the clothes pole that lifted the line up in the air and I might stand under the drips.

After such hard work we would have Graham crackers, Mama's favorite, and tea made in her little metal pot with the high up spout.

Some days Mama and I used to sift through her 'pieces'. She had all sorts of lovely colors and patterns, lots of them came from Carl's chicken feed bags. She helped me make doll's clothes. I learned to thread her needles, how to make stitches- they were never very fine and even like hers, and also she let me work the sewing machine to sew longer seams.

Or we might make butter out of soured cream that she put into a big jar with a lid and we shook it and shook it until little lumps of yellow appeared, they clung together into bigger lumps until suddenly, it came to butter- a big yellow mass floating in a whitish, watery milky stuff she said was 'buttermilk'.

Mama liked to pat and smooth the butter into a bowl. She took her time and did this carefully so it had a smooth and even top and set it aside in the ice-box or another cool place. Then she might set to and make buttermilk pap, which was a sort of sour sweetened milk pudding. Then we could have a feast especially if there was new bread too.

Sometimes we would make a surprise for the others coming home – cookies or a cake. The cake was often chocolate made with cocoa powder, or else yellow cake with extra egg yolks. If it was a yellow cake Mama had a special recipe for a see through frosting to turn it into June Bug Cake. I have never had it since and can't work out exactly how she made it but I think she used the eggs whites left from the cake mixture, with cornstarch, sugar and water and she cooked it on the stove until it was a thick see-through consistency – like frog spawn – and in it she put very big resins – these were the June Bugs. She poured it over the cooled cake, some of it stuck to the top but some also ran down the sides and collected in a pool on the plate beneath. I could run my finger along this and have a good taste without anybody really knowing.

As I got older and was not there to help, or maybe beg, Mama didn't do so much baking during the day. She sat in her chair a lot and once when she got up there was a big pool of blood. I thought she was bleeding to death but she said she was OK but would go and have a nap.

Chapter Eighteen

Starting School

I was to start school in September 1939 and Mama was going to make me a dress.

Carl collected as many of the 'calico' chicken feed bags as he could that had the same pattern. He worked on Land's End Farm for Mr. Clarke. It was an apple and chicken farm. So they had lots of feedbags. I don't know when the feed companies started making the bags out of 'stuff' that could be recycled into useful things but I do know we had a big pile of them but the trouble was in getting enough of the same pattern to make a dress with a full skirt. I knew what kind I wanted. It was pale yellow with Black-eyed Susan's all over it. We had one for a long time and I pestered him to get more. Then,

without me knowing, he must have gotten enough because one morning when I woke up there was the dress all made and lying on the sewing machine. I had new shoes too.

Nearly all summer we went barefoot. Many winter shoes

and boots were family hand-me-downs but buying new shoes for school had become, by the time I was nearly six, a ritual. Weeks before we stood on a piece of cardboard and Ma drew around our feet. Then she carefully cut around the outline and spent lots of time choosing from either the Sears Roebuck or Montgomery Ward catalogue. She put the cut out in with the order form and somebody went and mailed it. In a few weeks, or maybe even days, the new shoes would arrive in a box. They always fit. This year I was included in the school shoe ordering.

The school was about two or three miles from our house. All of the Rockies had gone there. It was just one room with two front doors and an entryway where kids hung their coats on a row of hooks. This entry also had a high bench with the pail of drinking water sitting on it. There might have been a cooking stove of some sort because we had hot cocoa in the winter. It was Land's End School and was built on a triangle of land down in front of Land's End Farm where Carl worked. How odd to call it 'Land's End' when it is perfectly clear the land doesn't end there. The land goes on and on far, far away, away past Hawleyville. Away further than I had ever been.

I had been to school with Tonie for special occasions and sat beside her at her desk colouring or 'working'. I remember one Valentine's Day when there was to be a party. I went with Tonie in the morning and stayed all day. I had a brown paper bag with my lunch just like everybody else. Tonie was by this time one of the big kids and I sat beside her. At that time the school went up to eighth grade; by the time I finished the highest grade was six. I guess she must have been twelve or thirteen and so I was two or three. I could just see over the desk, as my eyes were level with the lid. There was a sand tray on wheels at the back of the room and I was allowed to play in this with cardboard cut outs of camels and other strange animals. I remember being very quiet because Tonie said I had to. I also played with some very cold bricks in a small blue box. They were very pretty and smooth pale yellow, pink and brown and had arches and columns as well as various sized and shaped bricks. They were to become trusted friends by the time I went to school for real. This day I went out at recess with Tonie in the morning and had lunch with her and was fussed over by the older girls at lunchtime.

We ate from the paper bags and Tonie showed me how to unfold the bread paper from my sandwich and spread it out on the desk for a plate. After lunch we had scissors, paper and glue and bits of lace and ribbon to make valentine cards. I don't know who mine was for but it had a red heart carefully cut out by Tonie. Then we had the party with singing and games and food, all smeared together in a sticky memory. I was taken home to Mama; it is the first time I remember being away all day. We all raced home Tonie, Billy, Halsie, Jimmy and me to show off the valentines.

My actual first day at school was very different. Tonie, Billy and Hal had moved on to High School and went each morning on the bus. Jimmy and I were the only two Rockies going to go to Land's End. I had on my new shoes and dress. Jimmy was supposed to go with me but he tried to sneak away without me. He was caught and made to wait and go with me 'just for today', Mama said.

So off we set. He walked beside me or just in front of me until out of sight down the lane before he started striding on very quickly. We had been given some pennies to buy candy from Honan's Store; he stayed fairly close to me until then. After we left the store there were a few houses and then a bend in the road. On from the bend were, what we called, the 'flat'. It was a long section of straight road with no houses on one side and the Yaple's house set away back from the road on the other. There was woods and swamp on their side and empty fields across the road. Here Jimmy began to run on ahead,

stopping now and then to taunt me by allowing me to almost catch up before he ran quickly out of reach. When once I did catch him he hit me, knocked me down in the bushes then ran off all the way to school without me. I could hear the bell ringing and knew that, although Mama had seen that we started in good time, I was going to be late on my very first day.

I arrived crying and dishevelled with a cut on my leg dripping blood onto my new dress and my pants falling down about my knees. My lunch bag was torn and I must have made a sorry sight as I stood outside the door roaring with hurt and indignation. The teacher, new that day and just out of 'normal school' finally came and took me in. She didn't know who I was and I was sobbing too much to tell her. Jimmy wouldn't own me and it was one of the other kids who identified me as 'Rinkie Rockwell'. She looked on her list and found my name.

Oh yes, you must be Vera. Sit down there.

That is when I began to learn who Vera was supposed to be.

After that first day I liked school. The one room was divided into 'grades'. In my first grade there were just five of us. The rest were all boys. There were other girls older than I was and later younger girls came but I remained the sole female in my 'set'. As I was well used to boys I saw no real difference between the sexes and continued as I had always done to compete on equal terms in everything. I took my turn at filling the water pail from the pump at the side of the schoolhouse. We almost perfected drinking from our cupped hands, rubbing our faces clean and wetting our shoes in the process.

A pathway beaten by years of running feet went all around the school. In front was a hard packed earth play area. This was ringed by several old trees and beyond them leading down to the point of the triangle was a grassy meadow ending in a bog. By the time I went to school there were only about twenty-five children but I expect this was small compared to the thirty or forty it may have once held. The original building was covered in grey stucco cement, very rough and not nice to run into. My right temple had an almost permanent knocked patch where it hit the same spot in my clockwise tearing around the circuit. Outside to the left, opposite the pump side was a woodshed where we played with a ball. We used the shed as a backboard against which to bounce or else we threw the ball in endless games of 'overs'.

Ally-ally over.

Then when it didn't go over we shouted,

Pigs-tail!

Next to the woodshed were the outhouses, one for boys and one for girls. That was the real difference between us. I couldn't go in the boys one. A year or two after I started school the people at the farm planted a row of shrubs behind the outhouses to hide them from their view. These were great for hide-and-seek. There was already a big old maple tree behind the woodshed. The roots were exposed in a jumble of twisted walkways, seats and small caves. It was under this tree that I was to get my first teaching practice but that comes later.

Inside the school smelled like all schools do. There were blackboards on the front wall behind the teacher's desk and on both sidewalls between the windows. The room was furnished with an assortment of desks in graduated sizes that never quite corresponded exactly to the assortment of children in equally varying sizes and ages. These desks were mostly double ones and were normally separated into 'grades'; the youngest children had small tables at the front. We were promoted each year, which meant getting a table or desk the next size bigger in the relevant 'grade' or having your old desk moved 'up' in September. The grade immediately below mine had only one child, a girl. She often joined us.

There was no piano in the school but we did have a wind up phonograph. It sat in the front right corner beside the bookcase next to the flag. The record of 'The Star Spangled Banner' scratched out its tune every morning as we sang our tuneless rendition before we all turned to 'pledge allegiance' to the ' flag of the United States of America'. At first this was with our arms outstretched but I remember well when that was outlawed because of Hitler. And we had to learn to put our hands over our hearts.

Down at the back of the room were shelves and cupboards and the big sand table on wheels; it seemed to me as big as a bed. Setting out from the back wall, well into the room, was a new 'safety stove'. It was brown and had smooth straight sides that made a jacket around the fire. It was not a bit like our 'pot-bellied' Franklin stove at home. It was designed to allow the fire to be kept going all week merely by shaking down the ashes, topping up the coal and closing down the dampers. It was my brother Carl's job to see to the fire on Monday mornings and get it ready for the week ahead.

Miss Burr, being new, didn't know much about the fire and she had a hard job keeping it alight from day to day. So Jimmy would have to go on an emergency trip up to the farm to get Carl to come and 'see' to it.

Jimmy and I knew that the schoolhouse would be unlocked early on Monday morning and we eventually timed our arrival so that Carl would be gone and Miss

Burr not there yet. We let ourselves into the empty school and played about. Our delight was to rig up something to 'surprise' the teacher. On more than one occasion we secreted ourselves behind the stove and made a tower with the wooden play bricks that we knocked over whenever she arrived. I remember vividly the day I hid in the space under her desk, as quiet as a mouse, and tickled her ankles by 'walking' my fingers over her stockings. She yelled and jumped up on her chair, shouting at the mouse to go away.

On one midweek morning we arrived early, before Miss Burr's car was there. To our surprise the door was open. Inside Carl was standing at one of the side blackboards drawing an elaborate diagram of the stove and its stovepipe, damper and flue system. With numbered instructions labelled 'How To Keep The Fire Going Overnight', he filled the whole board with careful instructions. He read them out to us when he had finished and told us to tell the teacher to be sure to read it. We ran out to meet her car as soon as she arrived.

Lookie. Look at what Carl's done. You won't be able to let the fire go out now!

She left it up, un-erased, for a long time and we used to see her reading it now and then as she wrestled with the grate shaker. Miss Burr liked signs and labels and tags.

On my first day of school, once I had calmed down that was what I noticed. There were white labels on things. She must have put them up 'specially for me, I guessed. There had never been tags on things in the school before. Jimmy thought it was something to do with 'first graders'. He was right. I told Mama all about them but she didn't know. Pop thought they were probably some 'new fangled notion'.

Chapter Nineteen

'Reading, riting & rithmatic'

Once that first day finished I knew what school was about. We were supposed to sit still and be quiet. A new experience for me but Tonie had taught me what we were 'sposed' to do. There was another 'first grader' called Alec. He had been to kindergarten and he kept getting up to wander about and talk to people in a stage whisper that filled the room; I wanted to but didn't dare. Alec became a friend; his parents owned the chicken farm where Carl worked.

My memories of the six years spent in the one room school at Hawleyville are fused into a continuous ribbon of experience but I do remember learning to read; both times.

Our house had lots of books. My father loved books. From forever, I had wanted to learn to read. I carried books around 'reading' to my dolls and to anybody else with the patience to listen. Tonie used to sit with me behind the kitchen stove in the wood box. We would read. She read to me first of all. Soon I wanted a turn and she would read one page and then I would read that page back to her. We went over and over the selection of easy books in the house until I could 'read' them all as I pointed to each word with my finger.

She can read! Look Rinkie can read!

As indeed I could; but then she pointed to a word somewhere in the middle of the text which I couldn't name without going back to the start of the page and working my way towards it. When I got to the selected word I would pronounce it with great glee. The consensus of opinion then was 'Rinkie can't read; she's only memorised it'. Then there was a battle of opinions and I went storming away.

I can read. I can SO read.

Anyway, I continually followed people around with my book to ask 'What's that word' until, by the time I went to school, I could read all of the easy books in the house and there were few other books of which I could not read at least some. Sometimes I could find words I knew in Pop's paper and he set me to drawing rings around a particular word to see how many I could find. I felt very grown up when he did the count up.

In the weeks following my first day of school the labels and tags increased until the room bristled with white signs with black letters. They were bright against the oldness of the school walls and furniture. Almost everything in the school ended up with one of those white labels: table, desk, chair, floor, window, stove, blackboard, pail etc. Very soon all of us first graders and some second graders were herded everyday on a tour of these labels. Or else the teacher held up a card and we were to say the name and point to the matching label in the room. I was used to playing games at home and recognized this as a game. The rules seemed to be that the teacher pointed to a label and we all kept quiet until somebody made a hesitating guess then the teacher said 'yes' or 'no'. Or, we would have turns to answer. I liked games and learned this really well with lots of 'hummmms' and 'ummmmms' and wiggling about whenever it was my turn. Then I would make my guess in a tentative little voice or else a great whoop – like Alec always did when it was his turn.

I gauged my response on what the other kids did but soon caught on to the fact that the teacher liked it best if we actually said what was on the card. After some weeks of this game, Miss Burr called me up to her desk and asked me to name the words she had on a small set of cards. I got them all and she said, 'I think you can have a reader now'. She went and got the first 'Alice and Jerry' book. I had already seen it at home.

I can already read that.

I went through it like lightening. Then I went to the cupboard and got a whole pile of 'readers' I had been eyeing every since I got to school.

I can read these too.

She was too taken aback to say much. That was the first inkling I had that the flash card game was anything to do with reading. Rinkie and Vera caught up with each other. They could both read. It was not long before I was the acknowledged 'best reader' and in just a couple of years I 'took' the younger children for a reading group either in a corner of the room or out under

the big tree behind the woodshed. Johnny Seador spent as much time teaching me how to spit as I did teaching him to read but we both eventually learned. There was an art to spitting and having it land exactly where you say it will or, indeed, in working up enough saliva to have something to spit.

Reading was always to be a pleasure and a passion but spelling was a different matter. I just could not learn to spell. It is an affliction that has remained throughout my life. Letters come floating into words in the strangest order. It wasn't that I didn't want to learn. It was that no matter how hard I tried to learn; I couldn't. We always had a list of words to learn and I always tried to learn them. I never could. My heart pounds with remembered fear. I would think I had them letter perfect but, come the test, I got most of them wrong. The very worst thing was spelling bees. We all had to stand on our chairs, each to be given a word in turn. I crossed my fingers on both hands and crossed my toes inside my shoes that I wouldn't be 'down' first. When it got near my turn, heart pounding, I would take a deep breath and say any letter that came into my head, usually the wrong one. There were times when I did this even on words I knew. I made myself 'out' so I needn't suffer any longer and could pretend inside that I really knew the words but I just didn't want to stand on the chair any longer. My writing suffered because of the spelling but I was known as a story teller who would make up a tale on the least prompting.

Spelling was hard but arithmetic was easy. From very early days I was good at it and always got everything right. All of the grades were squashed together in one room so there was usually something interesting going on. I watched when the teacher taught the older children.

I can do gusintas. I can do gusintas.

I skipped my way home and landed breathless inside the kitchen. Pop was in his chair at the back of the table and Mama opposite. Warm bread smells tickled my nose.

I can do gusintas.

What's a gusinta? Bet you can't spell it.

Can too. G u s i n t a

Well what is it then?

I looked at Pop in disbelief. He knew everything.

You know a GUSINTA. 2 gusinta 4, 6 gusinta 12.

He picked me up and threw me in the air. It was one of the times I knew he was pleased with me and he must have been teasing when he pretended not to know. We had new arithmetic books with lots of pictures and funny questions. But I had learned 'gusintas' from listening to the teacher telling the older children. I learned lots of things that way.

Drawing was my best thing. Each September we started with boxes of new crayons. There were large sheets of blank paper and we were allowed to colour and draw whenever we had finished 'work'. I always finished quickly. One day Alec's mother, Mrs Clarke, came into the school. I think she may have been on the school board. I had done a drawing of two children standing on a hillside in the wind. You could see the wind blowing their clothes, hair and the grass in the field. The teacher had put it up in pride of place at the front. Mrs. Clarke was taken especially to admire it. She came and stood behind me as I bent over another drawing. 'That child should have art lessons'. The idea was firmly planted to grow many years later.

Miss Burr was new to teaching and new to the village. We shared our first day at school. Most of the older children had been in the school for several years. They knew how it 'worked' better than she did. For no real reason, paper spitballs would suddenly start bouncing all over the room. Or the whole school would erupt in a coughing spasm requiring that one by one we asked to be 'excused' for a drink. A favourite trick was for somebody to throw a blackboard eraser out of the window, making sure not to be seen, and then ask to be 'excused' to go to the outhouse. He would then appear with the eraser, 'Look what I found outside; I wonder how it got there.' The commotion this caused was the signal for another eraser to go sailing out and somebody else to ask to go to the 'outhouse'.

We were supposed to 'go' at recess time but if you really needed to you could ask during lessons. You had to stand up beside your seat and put up your hand. The teacher would then say, 'Yes you can go', without any request required. Early in my first weeks at school, it must have been a trying day; Miss Burr didn't say 'Yes'.
I stood up and waved my hand around and she told me to sit down.

I want to go.

No, sit down.

But I need to go.

SIT DOWN!

I protested again,

I need to go!

NO. SIT DOWN

I sat down and squirmed about a bit and then stood up again. She just ignored my frantically waving hand so I pulled down my pants and peed on the floor beside my seat, sat down again and got on with what I was supposed to be doing. Silence thundered. One of the older children was sent for the mop and pail. Miss Burr was red in the face and I just got on with my work. She always let me 'go out' after that. I thought it was silly that we had to ask.

Mostly, the kids who went to Land's End School came from families who had lived in Hawleyville for many years. There had been Rockwells at the school for over twenty years. However, there was the occasional child who came for a month or two and then moved on.

One such was a big boy who had been 'left back' in Sixth Grade and came to Land's End for the end of that repeat year. He was bigger than anybody else and caused chaos by beating up everybody in sight. At this time it was not the relatively inexperienced Miss Burr, but Mrs. Bell. She had taught many of my older brothers and sisters and had 'come back' to Land's End. Even she could not prevent him from sitting in school playing with his pecker behind the defiantly raised lid of his desk that stood isolated at the back of the room. We watched in fascination both the activity and the battle of wills between him and Mrs. Bell when, one day, she had had enough. I'm not sure if the school had a telephone by this time but eventually an official came from Newtown. The boy was taken away in his car and did not appear in school again. There were also two small boys who came for a while; they were brothers who were, it was whispered, 'simple'. They seemed to spend endless days standing at one of the side blackboards copying the numbers 1-100. I felt as sorry for them then as I do now.

We learned 'readin',ritin' and rithmatic', in my time there was never a 'hickory stick'. But Jimmy assured me that our big brothers had often 'got it' from Old Pat MacCarthy long before our time. I think Mrs. Bell must have been tempted a time or two.

From Carl on down for the next twenty odd years the one roomed school was peopled with ' Rockies' up through eighth grade, until Tonie, who finished seventh grade and then was bussed to Newtown. Jimmy saw another change and he was sent to Newtown after grade six. All my Hawleyville school years I spent at Land's end. 'Rockies' were all lively and somewhat headstrong – some more than others. Tonie, who was herself shy, recalls with some glee and a bit of vicarious pleasure:

"...when Jiggy was in about third grade he did something that angered the teacher He got whipped with the rod. Jiggy began to carry on something awful, kicking and thrashing, until he broke the metal part of the desk. Old PH, the teacher, came to whip him again and Jiggy grabbed his gold watch chain and broke it. Finally they both calmed down. Jiggy said he wasn't hurt much but just felt like paying him back".

This incident perfectly defines what is seen by some as a 'Rockwell trait' – an innate stubbornness, combined with self-will, tenacity and the certainty of being 'right' even when wrong. Certainly it describes my father who had such a bad temper he once smashed a whole hand of bananas - a rare, rare treat- and ground them into the cellar floor because the 'kids' had been pinching them behind his back. He, so some said, would argue 'black was white if it suited him'. So it's not surprising that at six I saw no alternative to peeing on the floor; I wasn't going to wet my pants. That would be shameful. I still think I was right!

Land's End School

Chapter Twenty

Measles

There was a day when the inside of the schoolroom began to spin and the floor wobbled. It was bright springtime and the sun lighted a dusty dance of tiny sparkles in its rays that slanted across the dimness of the room. I sit at my desk feeling sick. My head hurts. The room sways in waves of sickness as the walls fold in upon me. I want to go home but am afraid to ask the teacher.

Underneath the sick I feel hungry and I think about my lunch in the brown paper bag out in the passage. Whatever else it has in it I know there are, exceptionally, two big oranges. Oranges are a treat and to have two all to myself is extraordinary. It may have been a bribe because I was reluctant to go to school that day and 'not hungry' at breakfast. When lunchtime comes at last, I take out the two golden orbs all shiny and round, as big as softballs. I hold them for a long time one in each hand and feel their weight, running my fingers over their slippery skin with its dimples. The comparison with Mama's lost breasts is somewhere just below consciousness; I want their golden promise.

Fear and sickness shake my hands as I break the skin of one orange and tear the peel away. It is thick and pale yellow under the skin, my thumbnail digs away the deep pith to find the orange flesh. The colour burns into my eyes and the smell brings tears as the juice runs down my fingers. Suddenly my mouth tastes of water. I am not quite sick but I know I can't eat. Tears and frustration at the lost prize turn to anger; I feel wretched and give the oranges into somebody else's eager hands and ask the teacher if I can go home.

Not right now. Sit at your desk and put your head down; you'll feel better soon.

She has decided I must stay for the afternoon. So I sit there hunched over the desk with my head on my arms hearing the sounds of school

far away outside the lump of misery that is me. Voices are loud at first; then they echo like stones falling down a well rising and falling in time to the thundering in my head. I open my eyes; the shapes in the room swell and surround me to rise and fall away, recede and advance to the tune of the sickness which washes above, beside, over and inside from the outer edges of space. Suddenly I erupt. Floods of frothy sick splash over the desk, the floor and down my dress. She lets me go home.

I leave the crumpled lunch bag with the orange peel inside in the passageway. I walk home, hot and very thirsty with the salty taste still in my mouth. Beads of sweat run down my whole body before they turn into cold nauseous icicles. The sun makes black spots in front of my sore eyes as it beats down upon my hot head until that is the only warm part of me. I am now shaking and chattering, my cold body trapped inside the unreachable warmth of the sun. It merges with the lost oranges into hopelessness.

I must have roared and shouted because I remember the quietness afterwards and the feeling of being held, sobbing as I lay back on the bed. Mama had heard me and met me as I rounded the corner of the house. She cooled my head with a wet cloth and murmured something about measles.

I awoke to find the doctor leaning over me with a spoon in his hand. He parted my lips with the handle and looked inside my mouth. The doctor was never called unless somebody was really very sick. I was scared. 'Yes, it's measles', he said, ' white spots'. Now, even a very little child knows that measles is 'red spots'. It must be some awful kind of measles to have white spots and require the doctor. (Years later I was to learn about white Kophlic spots – the telltale diagnostic sign of measles.) Sometime a day or two after the doctor's visit I had a drink of milk and was sick. Out came white spotty lumps.

That must be the white spots.

Relief flooded over me. I would not die of the white spots anyway. I could see the red ones covering my arms and legs and belly just like measles are supposed to do and I settled down to itch and cough myself better.

I was not in my usual bed but in one of the two double beds in the alcove off the 'other room'. My father slept in the other bed. Mama had supervised the putting up of newspaper over the windows to darken the room. People thought light shining in the eyes caused 'measles blindness'. I could now read well and, when feeling better, spent much time perched up on the window ledge reading the yellowing paper on the windows. I also did colouring or cutting out things from the catalogue. I had paper dolls with lots of clothes. You used to get them in a book and you had to cut them out very carefully. My favourites were two tiny twin babies; I let them sleep in a pair of kitchen matchboxes and kept their clothes in the sleeve of the box.

A picture hung at the bottom of the beds in the alcove. It was the only real picture in our house. It was of a ring of children's faces – angels maybe – they had golden hair and pink cheeks. Each face had a different expression. The picture was dark and flyspecked with age and infestation but, nevertheless, the browns, yellows and dark blue of the paint seemed to glow in the half-light. I loved the children's faces and was at first content just to gaze at them. Then I started to tell them stories and made up stories about each of the 'angel faces'. Years later I was to see a picture like it in a London Museum but I never found it again. It had gone into memory of lost childhood like the faces that kept me company during measles.

Chapter Twenty-one

Winter

Winters in Connecticut were cold. Sometimes they were slow at getting started with a muddy, slippery not quite freezing beginning giving way to hard ground and frozen puddles that melted in disappointment by noon. Slight snowy showers fell but vanished into dampness. Morning would find the ground hard and steely with sharp ruts and a film of ice over the puddles too thin to be any use for sliding. A flurry of snow might fall and give false hopes of sledding. Nights were early and mornings dark. It took some time for everybody to get used to being packed together in the other room or the kitchen, the only two rooms that had heat. Like animals we had to get used to each other again.

Card games, discarded over the summer, came into their own again. Word games like 'Twenty Questions', 'I'm going on a trip' became rituals. 'Buzz', a counting game in which the number three, no matter where it occurred, was replaced by 'buzz' soon became too easy. Other numbers were then ascribed different sounds like 'knock' for five and 'zither' for seven. Thus counting past thirty became: buzz-one, buzz-two, buzz-buzz, buzz-four, buzz-knock, buzz-six, buzz-zither, etc. We once worked out a system where not only did you buzz on three and knock on five but on everything divisible by three and knock, I mean five. So you buzzed and knocked the number of times it was divisible. Thus counting from 20-30 went something like this: Knock-knock-knock-knock, buzz-buzz-buzz-buzz-buzz-buzz-buzz, 22, twenty-buzz,buzz-buzz, buzz-buzz-buzz-buzz-buzz-buzz-buzz,knock-knock-knock-knock-knock, 26,buzz-buzz-buzz-buzz-buzz-buzz-buzz-buzz-buzz,28,29,(then we were given a choice either ten buzzes or six knocks). It became very complicated and usually ended in a terrible argument.

We didn't have a radio until sometime in the early stages of the War. We had a wind-up Victrola and a small collection of records. Rinkie's favourites, which she sang at the top of her voice, included:

"Down by the river in an itty bitty pool,
Swam five little fishes and the mother fishy too
Swim said the mother fishy, swim if you can
And they swam and they swam right over the dam."

And

"I'm looking for the Olgol Polgol

The funny little Olgol Polgol

His mother was a pollywog, his father was a whale,

I'm going to put a little salt on his tail.

I'm looking for the Olgol Polgol"

Sometimes we marched around beating time to a march by Sousa. We sang a ditty to our favourite one:

Ohhhhhhhhhhh. The monkey wrapped his tail around the flaggg pole

And burnt his asssss hole on the flag pole.

Winter was the time for cocoa around the fire and for popcorn and cracking hickory nuts. Always, in the fall we gathered a milk churn full of hickory nuts. Small and green then but by winter dried enough to eat. We didn't know about walnuts yet, at least Rinkie didn't. So we expected to have to work hard to get at their meagre meat. We had flat iron and hammers and started up our own anvil chorus sitting in a ring around the stove. When we had enough shucks they made the fire blaze with blue and orange lights. Carl might make fudge; he was the expert.

This almost winter was the signal for Mama to try and find us all enough winter clothes. Growing seemed to be confined to summer and so there was a great trying on of clothes when the cold weather began. Sometimes a box came from the church filled with nearly new garments. Why did Mama cry over such delights?

When she was small Rinkie had a red snowsuit with a hood. It was only later that she wore a too small coat and the dreaded lisle stockings that had to be held up with dirty elastic garters that cut into her upper legs and gave her red welts. The stockings never stayed up. She hated them. I think she learned about the secret hide-away from Tonie whose place it really was. Down at the end of the drive where it met the road to Mrs. MacArthur's, the stonewall eroded into a heap of stones with small caves just right for concealing things. Rinkie had some socks hidden there and during one winter she stopped each morning on the way to school and changed into them leaving the long stockings behind until evening. She didn't care that her legs turned blue and her feet were wet and cold from trying to put on the socks without touching the snow. Some mornings the socks were frozen so she had to wear the long stockings anyway. Once she forgot to change back again in the afternoon and arrived home wearing the, by now, dirty white socks. Mama didn't say anything but the next morning Rinkie went off to school wearing a pair of boy's knickerbockers. It didn't matter that the crotch came down to her knees; they were long like the leggings other kids had and they didn't wrinkle. She wore them until the warm weather came. The secret caves between the stones were filled with other treasures; it was here she kept her stash of marbles and her clothesline skipping rope to protect them from the boys. Or even illicit candy bought on the way home from school with an appropriated penny.

For, if the truth is told, Rinkie was not a nice little quiet child. She had a rogue streak, wilful and stubborn and was sure she needed to be a part of everything, often in trouble. Not always of her own making, 'the boys' blamed her for everything.

Rinkie did it.

Didn't.

Did

Didn't

Did so!

One morning when everybody was getting ready for school, Rinkie became such a nuisance that Mama sent her back to bed. It was cold by then as they had been up a long time. She bawled and kicked her feet and pounded the pillows and the feather ticking to no avail. Mama didn't even notice. So she settled down and plotted revenge. That was when she peed in Mama's side of the bed and pulled the ticking up over it and made the bed up like it had not been slept in. She quietly got dressed and sneaked out into the by now quiet kitchen where Mama sat with her tea. All seemed to be forgiven and the real day began. By night time everybody had forgotten whatever incident had sparked the temper tantrum. When it was time to go to bed Rinkie was as surprised as Mama was to find the sheets frozen together with yellow pee.

I didn't do it. You must have peed in your sleep.

Mama's face, as she got clean sheets, didn't quite hide the sudden flash of laughter in her eyes. She knew and Rinkie knew she knew.

The winters of childhood are always covered in snow. New England snow, deep and white, magic with possibility and change when

even the backhouse wears a white cap and stands proudly black against the brightness. We had our own toboggan made from a metal roadside sign and the big boys made a toboggan run down the hill from the top garden, in front of the chicken coop, beside the barn and out into the road if we were lucky enough to stay on that long. A system of ropes gave it a curved up front and that was where Rinkie rode, between somebody's feet, whenever they let her, which was not always. We ran our run far into the night with shouts and laughter. In daylight the little kids were allowed on the road to sled. We had 'Flexible Flyers' with red handles. Rinkie was good at it even when just three of four. Because she was the littlest she often had a run down on somebody's back and then a pull up the hill again. But also, because she was 'the runt', she often got left behind and had to make do with sitting in a shovel with the handle through her legs to ziz-zag herself down the hill. If she had a sled she soon learned not to put out her tongue on the metal bar that held the handle to the wood otherwise it froze and stuck to the metal and she had to go home dripping blood.

When there was a blizzard the snowplough came and cleared the main roads. Then there might be drifts beside the road as much as five or six feet high. One winter Jimmy and Rinkie dug an igloo inside one of these in which they played for weeks until it finally melted.

The best winters were those that didn't start with snow. A clear and very cold spell resulting in a big freeze ensured that Upan's Pond became the centre of fun. The brook and the swimming hole seldom froze hard enough to walk on because of the running water. Upan's Pond was different. It usually froze solid. The first freeze was often not enough to make skating possible. There were rules. The ice had to be thick enough to hold the weight of one of the big boys jumping up and down and he must also be able to walk all the way across to the island or the other side with no cracks appearing. We often tested it much too soon and went home with wet feet. The sound of the cracks were as loud as gunshots to the ears of small fry trying not to let anybody know of their illicit pre- skating 'tests'.

There was only one factory in Hawleyville. It was Upham's Tea Factory. Mr. Upham owned the one big house in the village and the pond was inside these grounds. We were not to go there in summer but in winter he allowed the whole village in for skating. There were lights on wooden posts and he turned these on for the skaters but he, nor his family if he had one, never ventured out; at least, if he did we didn't know. Our family had a selection of 'clamp on' skates hardly known to modern kids even then. They were a metal frame that adjusted to size by a screw nut in the bottom and a sliding bar. In front and back they had cleats that clamped onto the shoe there was a strap that came over the ankle and a screw adjustment at the sides to make them stay on. Some were single runners and some had two runners. Two runners ensured that you could stand up easier but they only seemed to glide in a straight line. Single runners gave more scope for showing off. But both kinds were prone to falling off right in the middle of your best glide ensuring plenty of bumped heads and sore butts. The ambition was to have shoe skates and our family had some but only in big sizes. Not for runts. Rinkie got some for Christmas years later after she left Hawleyville but by then it was too late.

Skating was only really good if the ice came before the snow. Then, when it did snow, teams of kids would use brooms to sweep the ice and clear a path for skaters. Sometimes when the snow was very deep this was not possible and skating had to be abandoned until there had been a partial thaw and another freeze. Then the ice might have bumps of frozen slush in it waiting to trip one up or to become part of an ice jumping skate run.

Snowmen were, of course, winter playmates. We could roll them big by starting in the upper hill behind the house and working a zig-zag course going kitty corner downward to the kitchen door. One stood all one winter, much bigger than Pop, a silent sentry in the dooryard. He had coal eyes and a stick mouth and nose and a woolly hat stretched over his flattened cranium. A giant in the dooryard could be a good thing.

Winter wasn't all fun. We used to sit with our feet too near the fire, in fact with our feet on the rim of the stove when we could get away with it. Most of us had chilblains.

Pop suffered most of all. It was not unusual to find him sitting in the kitchen with his back to the stove and his feet in a pail of cold water. Or to see him suddenly jump up and take off his socks and walk barefoot all through the unheated rooms on the bare boards cooling his feet. As often as not he left all of the door open on his way.

Nobody ever shouted at him.

Shut that damn door!

One fearful night a commotion in the dooryard brought us all out into the cold to see Pop in his bare feet making holes in the snow as he yelled and called curses down upon all of our heads as if we were directly responsible for his chilblains. It did chill our hearts and we kept out of his way when he was finally calmed by Mama and brought sobbing into the house. He may have had a bit of firewater before this; sometimes he did.

Mama could be surprised at it fairly often. But, I only remember a few occasions when Pop cried. Once was a Sunday when a deep snowstorm prevented the Sunday School Bus from running. The church in Newtown ran a bus every Sunday. Pop often went to church; we always went to Sunday school. Mama stayed at home and cooked the chicken dinner. This day we were all ready when the phone rang.

There isn't any Sunday school. They bus can't get through.

Pop decided we would have the service in the other room. There were some neighbour kids who went too and they were at our house waiting to go with us to get the bus at Mrs. MacArthur's corner when he announced this. The kitchen chairs were brought into the front room and lined up in three straight rows. Then we all sat down, even Mama. Pop started the service. We had one or two hymns; Mama led the singing. She came from a singing family and her voice was very beautiful. She seldom sang now except to us kids or when she sat sewing or was busy in the kitchen. But when she was young she, and all of her sisters, her brother and her mother and father had been a choir of some distinction in their small upstate New York community. Her sister, Aunt Maude, was still active and was asked to sing solo in many of the churches in our part of Connecticut. This day, Mama sang in an unforgettable voice, as we had never heard her before.

After the singing, Pop said a prayer that seemed never-ending. Each time we thought it was time to say 'Amen'; he went on with another long passage. At last it came to an unexpectedly abrupt close. It was hard to follow the unfamiliar cadences of Pop's ministerial voice. There was another hymn followed by a Bible reading. Pop had out the big Bible with its important marker dramatically thrown back when he opened the book to read. He had a rich speaking voice and read aloud beautifully. An occupation too seldom indulged. This time he started with a beautifully ringing first passage, gradually as he became more deeply immersed in the words and less in the dramatic effect, his voice quietened and the words hurried into each other until he was reading with out thought or knowledge of our presence sitting in front of him on the kitchen chairs. Suddenly, he snapped the book shut and sunk to his knees sobbing, *'Why whenever I read it do I pick something that makes me not believe?'*

Mama quickly brought the service to an end and we went into the kitchen taking our chairs with us and started a subdued game at the kitchen table. The neighbour children went home. Pop soon emerged, flung on his coat and was lost into the snow. He didn't return until well after the chicken had been cooked and served. He ate his solitary way through the plateful Mama had kept hot in the oven. Was it this memory that caused him to hate the later popular song, 'Let it Snow, Let it Snow, Let it Snow'. He threw things at the radio whenever it came on.

Sometimes, towards the end of winter there would be a deep fall of snow followed by a slight thaw and then a big freeze. This made the snow crusty on top; often we could walk on it like walking in another world a foot off the ground. There were more times when the crust broke with every step and we sank in to our knees or crotch. Our family delivered the papers from Honon's store to the entire village. It was a job passed down from brother to brother. It was days like this, when bikes were no use, that Jimmy and Rinkie were asked to deliver the papers to the 'back road', the one past the railroad bridge with only four houses. Then it would take us about three hours to go the distance we could normally walk in about a quarter of an hour. We felt like heroes when we arrived at each house to be invited in for a warm drink, candy, cake or cookies and sometimes all of them. Maybe, if it had been really stormy we would have two days worth of papers and then we were doubly welcome since the telephone wires were sure to be 'down' as well.

Then one day would come the thaw to float rivers of mud everywhere, leaving behind grey patches of smutty snow to remind us of winter fun.

22 Chapter Twenty-two
Nearly no Christmas

Usually Christmas started early but everything was different this year. No pies baking. No cinnamon smells in the kitchen. Jimmy had been snooping about but he couldn't find anything hidden anyplace. Nobody even suggested they go and look for a tree. Jimmy had already found one up in the woods, a great big one, and Rinkie had found one in the back lot- a little one but quite nearby. It would have been just right. Nobody said there wouldn't be one but there just wasn't one.

Now it was Christmas Eve and Rinkie was in Mama's bed with Patsy. She had already told Patsy as much of "Tws the night before Christmas' as she could remember so she started again from the beginning:

"Tws the night before Christmas

And all through the house

Not a creature was stirring

Not even a mouse.

The stockings were hung

By the chimney with care......"

They had put the longest stockings they could find at the bottom of the bed 'cause they didn't have a fireplace, just a stove. She didn't know how Santa got out of the chimney but he had come last year so there must be a way. Jimmy didn't put his stocking with theirs. He was two years older and allowed to stay up. She snuggled down beside Patsy and when *she* got to "And I heard him exclaim as he drove out of sight. Happy Christmas to all and to all a good night" they were both still wide-awake and so they started to play the 'Are you sleeping?' game.

'Are you sleeping or are you awake?'

'I'm sleeping.'

'OK I'll sing to you.

"Up on the housetops,

Click, click, click.

Down through the chimney

With good St. Nick.

He has a dolly

And lots of toys

All for the little ones

Christmas Joys

Ho ho ho

Who wouldn't go.."

....

Are you sleeping or are you awake?'

'I'm awake.'

'OK I'll sing something else.

"Away in a manger

No crib for a bed

The Little Lord Jesus

Lay down his sweet head.

The cattle are lowing

The Baby awakes..."

Are you sleeping or are you awake?

Are you sleeping or are you awake?'

No answer, so she must be asleep. It was a game they'd played every night since Patsy had come to stay. Rinkie started it. She was Patsy's aunt even though she was just four years older. Mama said she had to look after her. She did feel sorry for Patsy but it wasn't fair for her, an eight year old, to have to go to bed at the same time as a four year old.

Tonight it was even more important. It should be Christmas tomorrow but it might not happen. Maybe Santa would not come. It could be that that's where Mama and Pop had gone - to find out. Mama never went far. She was always there but tonight they had been put to bed very early and the boys were in charge. Even her big sister Tonie didn't live at home anymore.

Rinkie tried once more. 'Are you sleeping or are you awake?' All was quiet. She got out from under the

feather bed quietly and carefully and crept into the kitchen. The lamp was lit but nobody was there. She could hear them in the other room. The boys were there, cracking hickory nuts and playing buzz with threes.

'One, two, buzz, four, five, buzz, seven, eight, buzz, ten, eleven, buzz, one-buzz, fourteen, buzz….. …'

They didn't see her come in and go to look at the pile of paper chains and lanterns she and Patsy had made – and the paper angel they had ready for the top. She didn't know where the glass balls were.

Halsie and Jimmy were up to the best part –'buzz-one, buzz-two, buzz-buzz when she appeared, suddenly, in front of them.

'Ain't we getting a tree?'

'No, Pop won't let us take the axe, or the saw. He said so. Buzz-four… buzz –off'

Tears came up and made the room all blurry. It must be the war – and because Sissie is an angel.

'I'm going back to bed.'

'Good riddance.'

The bed was still warm and Pasty asleep. She tried to wake her up but she wouldn't stir. Maybe Sissie will tell Santa Clause where Patsy is. Sissie was the first baby Rinkie could remember holding. At first she was just a bigger doll – still and asleep. But she grew and grew. The last time Rinkie saw her she was in her white long nightgown, pushing her legs straight and holding out her hands. Just like a little angel with bright, bright eyes laughing. Now she was a real angel, they said, and Patsy, who was Sissie's big sister, had to come and stay here with her Grandma because her mama and daddy, Martha and Joe, were both in a sanatorium with TB. Rinkie didn't know what TB was but it must be bad because Sissie had died of it. Nobody knew about it until it was too late.

'But we could've had a tree and Santa might find us anyway. We've got a chimney.

Maybe we should have put the fire out. Maybe that's what we should do. Then he can come out of the stove in the other room.'

Out she went again. Now the boys were in the kitchen popping popcorn. They were making strings of it using one of Ma's needles. They were laughing. How could they laugh? They let her string some too, but it was quite hard to push the needle through and they were much faster than she was.

'Give it here.'

'Maybe we need to put the fire out. Then Santa will be able to come down'

They just laughed and stuck out their tongues.

'Maybe he ain't coming. Go back to bed we're busy.'

Too scared now not to do as she was told Rinkie went away again into bed beside Patsy's warm back. She was careful to leave enough room for Mama. It must be because of the war, she decided. All the big boys were in the war. Tonie, her nearest sister, was at Mary's looking after Susan and Blanche because Mary had to work. When she remembered, all the other years it had been one of the big boys who got the tree, not one of those left at home now. Benny, Jiggy and Billy were in the navy. Johnny was just gone. Pop wouldn't let them use the axe, they said. But they always did what Pop didn't know about – like using his gun to go squirrel shooting. It was dark in the room but she could see a light outside. It was the lantern they used to go down to the barn to feed the cows when they used to have cows before the big boys went away to the navy. It shone through the feathery angel wings of frost on the window. She could hear Jimmy and Halsie laughing outside the window now. She jumped up and went to look. She had to scrape the white frost away. There they were and they had a tree- a little one – the one from the back lot.

Jumping into bed again, she patted Patsy's sleeping face. ' I'll sing you another song anyway', she said sleepily.

"Jackie Frost, Jackie Frost
Came in the night
Left the meadows that he crossed
All gleaming white."

She didn't know when Mama got back but in the night she knew she was there. It was Patsy she heard saying, "Rinkie, Rinkie are you sleeping or are you awake? " She opened her eyes. Patsy's face was looking at her so closely that their noses were touching.

'I'm awake.'

'Did Santa find us? I can't find my stocking.'

They got up. Mama was in the kitchen having tea. "Did he come?" Pop was grinning from his chair at the other side of the table. The boys were jumping up and down. 'Hurry up, come on. He's been'

They ran into the other room. There was the little tree all decorated with paper chains, the angel, popcorn and the glass balls. There were presents piled from the floor to the ceiling and right at the top were two big dolls that could reach out their arms. Best of all were new crayons and colouring books and Chinese checkers with a full set of marbles. The stockings were lumpy with candy and apples and an orange each. No coal this year. 'We must have been good', Jimmy shouted.

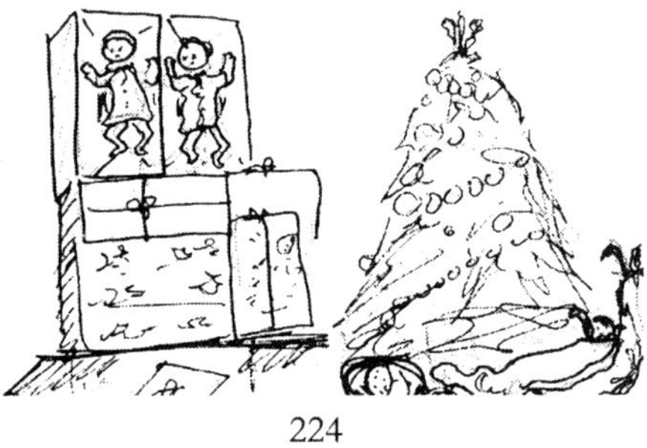

Chapter Twenty-three

Steam Heat

Far-away thunderclouds gather in a rolling grey rumble. Then comes a yellow smell heralding the storm.

Dusty feet pound across the dooryard in a tippy-toed dance. The chickens squat in their dust holes with feathers akimbo.

Run! Run! Run like stink.

Too late. Polka dots land on the red earth and plop into a timeless rhythm. Rivers of dust run off our dirty skin as we skip hand in hand in the warm, enwrapping ochre odour of summer rain in the dooryard.

On this day the rain came without malice, friendly and warm, turning the dusty air into a bath of joy. There is nothing more fun than to run free in summer rain, then to smell the fresh, wet earth when the sun comes out again.

Not all storms were so friendly. It had been hot, hot, hot for some days. We could feel the storm coming from afar. Loud thunder split the air with sudden slaps. Rinkie was frightened. Mama was sitting at the sewing machine in the corner of the kitchen nearest the door. She worked her feet up and down faster and faster as the storm got nearer. Rinkie wanted to get near to her, to sit on the treadle even, to have a ride but she had been told that lightening was attracted to metal. She wanted Mama to stop sewing but she was afraid to say so. Mama was in her own world anyway driving her machine like a team of horses.

Rinkie tried standing in different parts of the kitchen to count the time between the thunder and the lightening flash. Sometimes she only got to three. She didn't want to sit down because then she couldn't run. First she stood near Mama's chair but Mama was too busy to notice. Then she leaned against the shiny rail of the stove until she remembered that it was metal. So she moved across to the sink and stood watching Mama.

With a terrible suddenness, an almighty bang, the smell of sulphur and burning, a blue flash and tiny pieces of lino and newspaper whirled around her. Rinkie stood motionless as a red fireball bigger than a basketball danced around the kitchen, under the table and towards Mama and out through the open door.

We had been struck by lightning.

On the floor at the near leg of the stove was a large hole in the new lino. The newspaper underlay was burning and there was a scorch mark on the floorboards beneath. By now everybody was crowded in the kitchen and somebody had poured the bucket of water over the smouldering lino. The storm still raged. Rinkie was shaking and very quiet with terror but Mama didn't seem to notice; she was worried about the new lino. Mama told her to go to bed.

Lightning never strikes twice in the same place. It can't strike feathers; go to bed.

She stayed in bed until excitement overcame her fear and she ran out with the rest of the kids to see what other damage had been done. We discovered a scorch mark on the side of the house and the telephone wires had burned bit of the rubber that had coated the inner wire, in little burst pieces all the way along it. (For a long time afterwards Rinkie thought this was what Pop meant when he talked about a 'line storm'.) We followed the line down the driveway and found a new split and scorch marks on the telephone pole that had had the initial strike. It must have travelled along the line, through the telephone, which was burned out, and must then have jumped to the pot-bellied stove, along the stove-pipe and into the kitchen stove finally to discharge itself into the floor and produce the fireball that went to threaten Mama.

Rinkie was a hero. She was the only kid to be in the kitchen and to actually see the fireball. Mama had seen it too so Rinkie could not be accused of making it up as Jimmy thought. From then on, it took her a long time to be able to stay up during storms; she always took to the feathers to await the end, even when you could count to twenty between the flashes and the thunder.

In between summer storms the weather was usually hot. Then the iceman would come with his dripping load in the back of his red pickup truck. He expertly cut off a chunk and using his ice tongs carried it into the kitchen to refill the icebox. If we were lucky and he was in a good mood he let us use his pick to hack off little slivers and we had summer icicles to suck. By evening on a summer day the morning cows' milk would already be 'off', if we had run out of ice as we usually did. Then it was that Mama made butter and what she called 'buttermilk pap'. I have never discovered quite what this was but it had a strangely sharp taste and the consistency of a milk pudding. Rinkie loved spooning it out of a bowl with new bread. Rinkie loved pudding anyway.

One summer evening, we had ice and the milk was not sour so to use it up Mama made chocolate pudding for supper. She put it in a big flat pan outside the kitchen door on the stonewall fence behind the oil drum to cool. Rinkie helped to stir it and supervised the balancing of the pan on the rocks. So she just had to check on it to see if it had turned to pudding or was still runny. Several times she climbed up to stick her finger in the edge, each time it was still hot and runny but she licked her fingers clean and tried again in a few minutes. At last it was ready and this time she took a little handful but she slipped and slid off the rocks with the pan following. Chocolate pudding sprayed everywhere and

mixed with her tears and dusty skin to turn her into a sticky mess.

Look what Rinkie done. The little brat. Now we ain't got no puddin..

Somebody washed her down with a bucket of water. They were real mad at her. The other kids often blamed things on her that she didn't do; this time she knew it was her fault. But it wasn't her fault the lightning had nearly hit Mama. But it could have been.

There were some things that didn't seem to be anybody's fault. One hot day one of the Lattin girls came to get Mama to go and help her mother. Teddy was sick, very sick and they thought Mama would know what to do. We never saw Mama move so fast as she hurried down the path behind the house. We didn't have to be told not to follow. She was gone a long time and when she came back she was white and quiet. She talked to Pop on the rock outside in the dooryard far into the night. Rinkie went to bed by herself.

Rinkie knew that talking on the rock was serious grown-up talk. She had once listened to them talking about a baby, Mama had cried and Pop sat with his arm around her, a lost baby. Rinkie had been only little then and she knew SHE was the only baby so she decided the 'lost baby' might be her but she wasn't lost so it couldn't be. It was serious she knew but she didn't know why. Maybe Teddy might be 'lost'.

He nearly was. He had had convulsions and Mama had wrapped him in cool wet sheets. Then the doctor came and took him to hospital. He had polio and was paralysed. After that we couldn't leave the property for three weeks. We were in quarantine and had a sign on the tree at the bottom of the driveway. No swimming even. Nobody knew what caused polio and they thought it might be because of germs from the dump beside the railway near to the Lattin's house. So they brought some monkeys to live there to find out if they would get polio but they didn't. There was one other time we had been in quarantine with suspected scarlet fever. Pop hung up sheets in the other room to keep the germs confined and we had to stay indoors or on the property. It lasted a long time and Rinkie and Jimmy set themselves the task of reading the Bible from cover to cover. The Bible was quite hard to read especially the Chronicles; Rinkie always insisted that she 'read it all the way through' but I suspect she didn't. 'Scarlet fever' turned out to be a false alarm and it was deemed we had 'scarlatina' instead, though they seem to be one and the same thing. Maybe we just had sore throats and a rash.

We were often scratching, especially in the summer. Mosquitoes pursued us as we chased lightning bugs in the grass or even when we didn't. Lightning bugs didn't bite. They didn't even burn; they just flashed in the long grass in the summer night. We caught them and put them in a jelly jar with holes in the lid.

How many we got?

Twelve.

We need thirteen. We gotta get one more.

Hey. Don't let um out. Keep the lid on.

I'm just countin' again.

I told you we got twelve; now we only got ten.

Ok we so need three more now.

When we had enough we put the lid on tightly and put the jar in the dark to see the bugs blinking on and off. In the morning Rinkie looked in the jar.

Come 'ere. Look at this!

Where they all gone? There's only four left.

They must'uv ate each other.

Sure enough there were only four bugs inside the jar and all along the bottom were black specks, which we decided must be their eyes.

I guess they don't like eatin' eyes.

I guess.

Summer brought some worse bugs that left black specks on the feather ticking, mattresses and pillows. Bed bugs emerged to plague our lives in the steamy heat of summer. We would wake up scratching with bloody scabs on our faces and body where we had been bitten. I think they were around all of the time but it was in the summer heat that we suffered most.

Chapter Twenty-four

Bed Bug Day

Rinkie lay almost still in the bed on top of the feather ticking, scratching her bloodied arms and neck now and then. The heat was already closing in, pressing down on her sweaty face and nearly bare body. She listened to the far away sounds of something happening. Mama must have got up without her!

She listened harder and she could hear Pop yelling at the boys to 'Get the hell down there'. She couldn't remember how she got in bed 'cause she was going to sleep outside in the night. It was either mosquitoes or bed bugs and I guess the bed bugs won.

Rinkie crept into the kitchen; nobody was there but she could see that breakfast was finished. The fire in the stove was roaring. It was so hot she thought the bread might toast by itself. She helped herself to bread and runny butter sprinkled with sugar and ran out to see what was happening. Mama was setting out the washtub and washboard with lots of soap on the wooden bench by the kitchen window. Pop had sent the boys running down to the brook with pails and cans to collect water. He filled every cooking pot with water to heat up on the stove.

It must be bed bug day! Is it bed bug day?

Yes, get outta my way it's bed bug day. We're gonna get them damn critters

It happened almost every summer. It took all day; the campaign against the army of bedbugs that inhabited every crease and crevice of our mattresses and pillows. Pop organized it and everybody had to help. First the water was fetched and as much heated as possible. Then every item of bedclothes was put in the wash. It was the only time all the 'linen' was changed at the same time. Mama stood all morning at her washtub scrubbing. We helped with the rinsing and with wringing them. To do this one child got on either end of a sheet and one twisted it one way and the other the other way until we had it twisted as tightly as it could go and water stopped dripping. More than once we had to rinse it again because we had dropped the sheet in the dirt in this laughing process. Then it was our job to take the newly washed sheets and spread them out on every available patch of grass to bleach in the sun and to dry. Rinkie loved to shake the

sheets with somebody else on the other end to see them billow up and then settle on the long stems of grass and meadow flowers. Pop had scythed the longest grass into hay still lying thickly where it fell. Bed bug day was always sunny and hot.

A small army of boys made trip after trip upstairs to carry down the mattresses and pillows from the row of iron bedsteads that filled the upper story of the house. The four double bed mattresses from the downstairs rooms were manoeuvred out through the kitchen and carried up the hill. Once the bedding was all outside the attack began. We knew about the black specks that made trails along the seams of the mattresses and feather tickings but we seldom saw the bugs since they usually operated at night.

I seen three hundred running along this one.

I seen three thousand!

Com' on let's get them.

Armed with bug sprayers loaded with insecticide and, if we ran out of that kerosene, we helped in spraying the bugs and shrieked to see them running out of the bedding in panic. We sprayed and sprayed with the smell of chemicals deep in our heads and our hands working the pumps at a furious rate. Less fun was the job of washing down the floors under the beds, the springs and the bedsteads themselves with Lysol and water. It took nearly all morning to get the mattresses out and sprayed; us littler ones might be spared the washing down and be allowed to go swimming. Once everything was clean Mama had a rest and her cup of tea. Pop and the kids went swimming to take away the dust, itching feeling and the smell of bug killer. The bedding stayed outside until the evening sun began to cool. Then the boys carried everything in again and we helped Mama to make up all the beds with their clean sheets. The sheets were always stiff as if they had been starched and were almost as smooth as if they had been ironed. We learned that the more you shook them like sails when you spread them out to dry the smoother they dried.

Tired and happy to sleep in peace we lay down on fresh grass and flower smelling sheets, mixed in with the smell of Lysol and bug killer, looking forward to a scratch- less night with the only bites coming from the odd mosquito. The summer ritual had ended.

I'll tell you the tale of the bedbugs from hell.
They bit you and sucked you and made your limbs swell.
They marched on their stomachs and then upon us.
Those blood sucking critters, how they made us cuss.

So it's bed bugs and Lysol and freshly mown hay,
We're blasting those buggers; they won't go away.
It's bed bugs and Lysol and scrubbing all day.
We'll get them damn critters; we'll chase them away.

In winter the frost came, the windows to ice.
Pee froze in the pot; it was not very nice,
But those blood -sucking critters did not like the cold.
So it's of the hot summer this tale will be told.

Around about June, the first signs did appear

A crop of red spots on the baby's left ear.

They crawled from the ticking, from mattress and sheet

Up over the pillow and under your feet.

T'was on the fourth of July that they tested their might

The fireworks were over, we lay out in the night

Forced from our beds by the strength of their jaw

We lay in the dooryard on bundles of straw.

The morning came quickly in wet waves of heat

Pop shouted and cussed, he wouldn't be beat.

He got us all up with a great cry of, 'Shit'

'We'll get the damn bastards with doses of Flit'

An army of boys charged away up the stair,

To bring the damned bedding out in the fresh air.

The sheets they were washed and spread out on the hill

We'll get the damned bastards if we have the will.

Johnny and Jimmy went down to the store.

We had a Flit gun but we needed some more.
They got half a dozen and plenty of Flit
We sprayed bugs all day 'till the lantern was lit.

.

Ten mattresses lay in a row on the ground
Us kids with the Flit guns went dancing around.
Bed bugs came running from out of each stitch.
'We'll get you; we'll Flit you, you son of a bitch'.

The bedsteads were sprayed and the rafters and all
With elbow grease, soap suds and tons of Lysol.
Spare a thought for the dog and maybe the cat,
'Cause the kids and the Flit guns were equal to that.

Now evening comes and the house is put right,
Sleepy heads cradling down for the night.
Our sheets dried on flowers and newly mown hay
The Lysol and Flit chased the bugs all away.
So it's bed bugs and Lysol and freshly mown hay,

We've blasted those buggers; they've now gone away.

It's bed bugs and Lysol and Flit guns all day.

We've got them damn critters; we've chased them away.

I've told you the tale of the bedbugs from hell.

They bit you and sucked you and made your limbs swell.

They marched on their stomachs and then upon us.

Those blood sucking critters, how they made us cuss.

Chapter Twenty-five

The Forth of July

Usually, when Rinkie was small, there was a 4th of July picnic. Everybody tried to come home for it. More than any other, the Fourth was the summer day that held together childhood.

The candy case at Honon's now held even more exciting goods – firecrackers that came in all sizes from little 'put-puts' about an inch long and the size of a match that were all strung together into sets of ten or twenty with just one fuse, to ones as big as shotgun bullets. There were sparklers, roman candles, Mt. Vesuvias', skyrockets, Catherine- wheels, cherry bombs and other exciting ones I can't name. We let them off whenever we thought we might not get told off but the main show was held at night as soon as it was dark enough and before us little kids got to sleepy to care.

It was the 'put-puts' and the sparklers I was allowed to light. Jiggy could do magic with a few 'bullet' sized firecrackers and a row of tin cans. He hid the firecrackers underneath the cans and somehow connected them in tandem with fuse string soaked in kerosene. He'd light it and run shouting

Get out of the way you dumb kids!

Firecrackers and tin cans came exploding after us as we ran every which way. Some of the cans went shooting way up above our heads. Occasionally the big boys got torpedoes. These were used on the railroad to signal trains to stop. They were small red gunpowder cases that were strapped to the rail with two lead straps. Somehow they got hold of some and threw rocks at them to detonate a big explosion. I don't know if Pop gave them a licking for it, or even if he knew. How could he not know? Maybe it was him who brought them home anyway.

For the picnic we had long tables, set up onto saw horses, borrowed from the firehouse along with extra chairs and put out under the maple trees. Everybody tried to come home for the picnic. The Waterbury kids came in the back of Libby and George's pickup truck. They had blankets and pillows so they could sleep on the way home after the long, long day. Libby was the oldest girl and she always called Rinkie, 'Babe'. She already had two children by the time I was born and two more in quick succession. That made Rinkie 'Aunt Rinkie' as soon as she was born. By the time she was six or seven, Rinkie was 'Aunt' to several others as the older children married. They all came to the picnic and we had lemonade, watermelon, hot dogs and home churned ice cream, potato salad, cold cuts and more and more and more. The table was covered with food because everybody brought something. Cold root beer was brought out from the cellar with hard cider and beer and, I guess, some stronger stuff for the men. The washtub was filled with ice and this kept the bottles cold.

There was baseball, croquet, and general running around before going off to the swimming hole. We couldn't wait for night for the fireworks and somebody was forever setting off a small explosion. Hal, Billy and Jiggy were the experts in putting a 'cherry bomb' under a tin can to send the whole thing flying up into the air. Much less dangerous than Jiggy's firecracker experiments when cans flew in all directions. Cherry bombs were more predictable.

At night we had Roman Candles and Catherine Wheels and Sparklers for us little kids. As the last sparks flew away and the stars twinkled, the grown-ups sat and talked, Johnny might get out his harmonica and play. We rubbed sleepy eyes and fought to stay awake until we either lost the battle or were carted off to bed. Betty, Barbara, Lee and Annie would be put to sleep in the back of the truck to go home to Waterbury. George, Maggie and their kids lived in Hawleyville and they could walk home, so did Mary and Don with their babies, Carl and Rainy too. Then the war came and things began to change. I don't know when the last picnic was maybe about 1941 or 42. The older boys were in the Navy. Suddenly like the 'nearly no Christmas' there wasn't a Fourth of July picnic. In 1944 the family gathered for a different occasion.

Chapter Twenty-six

August 4th 1944

There were only three of us kids left at home Hal, Jimmy and Rinkie. Billy, Jiggy and Benny were in the navy. Libby, Mary, Martha, Carl, George and Johnnie were long gone from home. Tonie was now married and she had a baby and another on the way. In fact, Rinkie had been really disappointed at Christmas because Tonie was going to come with her baby, Georgie, ten years younger than Rinkie having been born in August 1943, but Rinkie awoke on Christmas Day scratching. She had chicken pox. They were afraid the baby would catch them. So the celebrations had been subdued. Not cancelled like the 4th of July picnic but quiet. Now there was some talk about Libby being sick and maybe that was why there had been no family get-together for the 4th.

Rinkie got up that morning, a little bit sorrowful but also quite excited. Mama and Pop were going away for the day on the bus to Waterbury to visit Libby. Mama almost never went away from home. They were leaving her behind with Jimmy and Hal. It is the first time Mama had left her on her own like that. Rinkie planned to surprise her and clean up the kitchen and do the dishes. She was nearly grown-up; she would be eleven in October. I think she went swimming in the morning but afterwards she put her plan into operation. It was really hot both inside and outside. Flies buzzed in the kitchen and the flypapers were full of dead ones. She heated water to do the dishes on the kerosene stove that they used in the summer. The butter was in a runny pool in the dish and there were lots of dishes scattered around the table where people had helped themselves all day. Wouldn't Mama be happy with her? She even swept the kitchen floor and set the chairs straight around the table. There was a pair of boy's pants on the back of Mama's chair where she had put them to remind her to mend them. Rinkie left them there where they were. She had just managed to finish the chores and was going out round the corner of the house to join them at the swimming hole, when she heard Jimmy crying from a long way away.

What's happened to him?

Rinkie set out on the run to find out. Thoughts flew through her head in tune with her flying feet. She remembered the time she had cut her foot on glass in the swimming hole and she had had to be carried home crying to have it soaked in Lysol and bandaged with old sheet. She rounded the corner of the drive and saw them all coming towards her. Jimmy was crying but he wasn't bleeding. She saw Pop and Hal and Jimmy and LIBBY but Mama wasn't with them.

Where's Mama? What have you done with Mama?

She really didn't have to ask because inside she knew. They told her the facts. Mama and Pop had gone to see Libby and when they were coming home they had to rush to catch the bus. Pop and Libby hurried on to hold the bus and Mama struggled to keep up. She called out to them to wait then collapsed in the street and had to be helped inside an air-conditioned store. She died quite quickly from either a heart attack or a stroke. Rinkie was never sure which. So Libby came back with Pop on the next bus and they had stopped on their way to collect the kids from the swimming hole.

There are lots of things during the next few days Rinkie was never quite sure about. She had never been away from home overnight on her own; once she had been taken by Jiggy on his grocery round to stay overnight with Mary but she had been so homesick by bedtime that she had had to be taken home again. Once when she was little Mama took her, Jimmy, Halsie, and Billy on the train to visit her mother in New York State. They had had to change trains in New York and take the Staten Island Ferry across the river. Mama had nearly lost one of the boys who went the wrong way in the tunnel. She threw the rest of us up against the wall and threatened us with a finger while she tore off after him. On the boat we stood at the rail and watched when a man lost his hat, which floated down the river. We watched until it disappeared into the distance. We stayed in Grandma Carl's house and went across the road to Uncle Ike's farm but Rinkie slept with Mama. That had been a long time ago. She had never slept anywhere but in bed with Mama. Now, when it was dark and the lamps were lit, Rinkie protested when it was suggested she go to bed.

I want to sleep with Mama. I want my Mama.

She remembers the exchange of looks. Libby tried to comfort her.

I'll be your Mama tonight.

OK

Rinkie was taken sobbing to bed, she fell asleep but woke again to an empty bed and voices in the kitchen. That was the end of crying. She knew Mama would not come back now. Nothing was ever the same again. It was an abrupt weaning.

It had been Patsy's birthday. She had been four on August 4th as she reminded everybody. Rinkie asked her the next day if she knew what was going on.

I know something has happened to grandma.

Rinkie was suddenly grown up and told Patsy the facts. They were sitting down in front of the house near the swing tree.

Grandma died; she won't come back now

They both knew about death because Sissy had gone to be an angel. The next few days passed in a jumble of sharp clear memories interspaced with a complete loss of recall. Rinkie and the boys were taken to Newtown to the pictures. She could never figure out why.

Mr Honon's funeral parlour was in Newtown and that is where she next saw Mama. Not her real Mama but a dressed up Mama lying in a strange bed- like box with her hair all combed and clutching a wilting bunch of pansies. Mama had a round pansy bed in the dooryard and we had been sent to pick the biggest bunch we could; these must be them. On the morning of the funeral we had to pick another bunch and not let Pop see us doing it.

At the funeral itself Rinkie wanted to sit next to Tonie. Tonie had always been a second 'mama'. Rinkie sat beside her and watched the huge bump that was another baby on the way. It was hot and the chairs were hard and everybody looked strangely clean and in unaccustomed shoes. She remembers acutely wanting to be the baby inside the bump. Everybody cried but Rinkie can't remember if she did or not. She can't remember much more about that day or the ones immediately afterward. It was a family get-together without the picnic or the fireworks. There were lots of people there she didn't know and she guesses Aunt Maude, Mama's sister who lived a few miles away, must have been one of them but she doesn't know for sure.

Rinkie can remember lots of things from the next year when she stayed at home with Pop, Hal and Jimmy but try as she will she can't remember anything about the next Christmas; it must have been cancelled.

Chapter Twenty-seven

The Line Storm

Mama was buried under the trees in the cemetery upon the hill behind the school. Rinkie could go and look at the scar in the ground and sometimes she did on the way home from school. But her Mama wasn't really there. At least she couldn't feel that she was. She wasn't at home either. Pop had left the boys pants where they were on the back of Ma's chair in the kitchen waiting to be mended. Once Rinkie found Pop leaning on them crying; she didn't know how to do mending.

The days and weeks and months after she died are jumbled together into an untidy tangle. In Mama's room there was a bureau and the top drawer was full of things we were not suppose to have. She never said we couldn't but we just knew with the wisdom of childhood they were somehow sacred.

Now it was my room because we had always slept together. She was gone and how could she look at her treasures now? Of course I had looked before. Whenever the opportunity came I edged the drawer

open and sifted through what was there. So I knew about the box of chocolates. A red heart shaped box with a satin red bow. The cellophane, until recently, had not been broken. One of the boys had sent it to her, or maybe brought it to her, from wherever he was posted in the Navy.

'It's too pretty to open', she had said at the time. It was ages before we discovered where she put it. Now it lay there accusingly. Little mice people had broken in and nibbled the edges; we had had some trouble in making it look like it had never been opened, I remembered. That summer had been hot and the candy was now misshapen and had that white bloom that comes on chocolate too long uneaten. It didn't even taste very good anymore. I can't believe that we didn't eat it all anyway but it is one of the tangled memories that remains snarled in that knot of grief. I was almost 11 and Jimmy 13. Hal was 17 and he soon left to join the navy. It was Jimmy and I who rummaged in her things.

Her engagement ring was in a small royal blue velvet ring box with a domed top and a pearl clasp. You had to pull quite hard to open the box. I had never seen her wear the ring and wondered how it could ever have fit her puffy fingers. It had three opals and four tiny diamonds. One of the opals has now fallen out but that happened much later. There was also a photograph of Mama and Pop together. It may have been a wedding photo but her dress was dark so perhaps not. In any case the beautiful young girl standing regally next to her handsome partner bore no resemblance to my Mama as I remembered her.

Did we find a key in the drawer? Is that what sent us upstairs to open up her trunk?

The day was hot. The house was empty except for the flies that buzzed everywhere, nobody to know what we were up to. The trunk, black with a dome top, sat in the middle of that un-floored part of upstairs one could reach only by balancing across the rafters on tippy-toe. We had often been up there alone and often tried to lift the lid of the trunk. This time we succeeded in getting it open.

It was heavy and we were covered in sweat and dust when the lid came up on its rusty hinges, slowly at first and then much too fast so that it suddenly banged open scaring us into giggles. Inside, on the top, was a white sheet covered with rusty reddish marks where the hinges had pressed. Jimmy opened the sheet and very carefully unfolded a long creamy, once white dress. It was heavy, with 'leg of mutton' sleeves, and it seemed to be entirely covered with white raised embroidery. As he lifted the dress out of the trunk it disintegrated into a mass of holes that grew as we watched the tiny moth carcasses fall away with the eaten cloth. By the time he dropped it back into its shroud it was just a heap of holes held in place only with the embroidered strings of flowers. We pushed the lid shut and never looked in the trunk again.

This happened quite soon after her death when there was nothing to do but snoop or fool about. In early September Rinkie went back to Lands End school for the sixth grade; Jimmy travelled to Newtown on the school bus. He was too old for Lands End.

Carl and his wife, Lorraine, Rainie as we called her, now lived in a house just further up from the cemetery, near the schoolhouse and the farm where he worked. They had two girls, Helene who was three or four years younger than Rinkie, and Carol Ann, who was little more than a baby. Helene looked so much like Rinkie that she once saw a picture of Rinkie holding her as a baby and said, 'Who is that baby I'm holding?' Carl worked for the Clarke's on Lands End Farm as he had done since he was fourteen or fifteen. He always said he caught Bob Clarke's college education as they sat together candling eggs, a slow process of holding each egg up before a light to check for imperfections. They listened to classical music and discussed life, philosophy and politics.

Sometimes Rinkie went up there; she loved playing with the kids. Rainie would give her supper often. Carl tended the graveyard, just as he kept in the fire at the schoolhouse. It took Rinkie a long time to get his joke: 'It's the best job I ever had. At least they never come out and complain at my mowing'

Rinkie loved to work Rainie's washing machine. It made a lot of sloshing noises as the central paddle rotated in the tub. There was a wringer attached and you fed the clothes in but you had to be careful not to get your fingers caught. She was old enough to do it but Helene had to be watched she didn't wring her fingers. Carl had electricity and you just snapped the light on and off.

At home we still had to light the lamps and now that Ma wasn't there the chimneys were usually blackened with smoke. The dishes always needed to be washed, as did the clothes. I guess we sometimes washed clothes at Carl's in Rainie's washing machine that year, but not always. I think also we sometimes sent a bag of washing to the laundry but I may be mixing that up with life at Tonie's on the farm. Pop didn't often light the kitchen stove except in really cold weather so we cooked on the oil burners and washed in a tiny basin full of water. Rinkie's hair was long and she couldn't do the braids tight enough for them to stay in all day and the boys didn't like to do them and Pop didn't always have time, besides he took too long as he combed and combed and stopped midway with tears in his eyes. So she got into the habit of going every morning up over the bridge and up the hill to the Lattin's where their mother braided her hair along with her girls, Isabelle, Mary, Flora and Rosie. Rinkie then walked to school with them.

Sometimes Rinkie stayed overnight with Isabelle and the other girls;

she loved to listen to their mother reading aloud at bedtime, 'Little Women', 'Joe's Boys' and the rest of Louisa May Allcotts' books. Not that Rinkie couldn't read them by herself, she just liked the feeling of being read to. Occasionally their father came home having had too much to drink, and then Rinkie hid under the bed with the other kids and listened to him make exaggerated threats and claims about what he was going to do. 'I'm going to kill you', seemed almost comic in his singsong drinking voice. We thought we knew it was just talk but we stayed under the bed anyway.

Most often she went home when the reading was done. But unless Jimmy came for her she was afraid to go over the bridge in the dark. Rinkie had always gone to play with Isabelle, Mary, Flora, and Rosie. So coming back over the bridge at dusk was not a new thing; she had always been a little afraid of some nameless terrible troll who might pop out and chase her. So two or three of the girls would start off with her as far as the bridge, they would all run across and then, feigning fear, the others would make Rinkie come back with them across – then they did it all again until finally they all went to the middle of the bridge together and turned and ran, feet pounding, to arrive panting at their own dooryard. This had been going on for years, even before Ma died. Now Rinkie went home accompanied by a dark nameless fear even in broad daylight.

Pop worked shifts so he often wasn't there in the evening or sometimes he was away all night. Hal, Jimmy and Rinkie looked after each other. Hal was the oldest and I guess he was supposed to be responsible. He was, as near as I can work out, about seventeen. Jimmy was thirteen and Rinkie ten and would be eleven in the October.

Pop was working when a great storm blew up in the fall after Ma died. I think it was a hurricane but Pop called it the 'line storm' because it was near the equinox.

We watched the sky become yellow, the colour of snot when you've got an old cold. It grew lower and lower to silently cover everything in a coat of gloom. The air closed in and around us trapping us in the house. Thunder rumbled closer and closer. Rinkie was scared. We lighted the lamps, all of them. We sat on Pop's side of the kitchen table in a row and listened to the wind 'getting up'. It rounded the corners of the house pelting rain onto the windowpanes. It shook the house then went away again to come tearing back even stronger than before. We put a chair against the door in case it blew in. The dog cowered under the table; he didn't need to howl; the wind was doing that. The lamps flickered every now and again when a gust forced its way through any opening it could find. We turned up the wicks but that just made the lamps smoke so we turned them down again. The telephone gave a brief ring but when we answered it the line was dead.

Must'tuv been struck by lightning.

Wind blew the line down more likely.

We could get struck by lightning.

Naw..you already been..It don't strike twice in the same place.

Rinkie wasn't so sure.

We'll maybe get hit by a tree.

She was so afraid that they didn't tease her anymore but decided to be reporters and use Pop's typewriter to make a newspaper reporting the storm as it raged. We sometimes heard the shipping news on the radio but it wasn't working now; no batteries I guess. We put in a bit of geography about winds sweeping the coastline but mostly we 'reported' local happenings.

In our newspaper storm the wind blew at over three hundred miles an hour. The rain filled the brook so it wasn't only the usual cowshit that floated down into the swimming hole but cows as well. The roof blew off Mrs.Jilson's barn and landed on her chicken coop; the chickens got carried clear away and floated down the hill on a river of rainwater. Mrs. Miller who was really a witch lost her broomstick. Whole lines of trees and telephone poles were uprooted and lay scattered like kindling wood over the whole of Hawleyville.

Outside the real storm raged and crashed and blew at the house trying to put out our lamps. But we were safely inside in the circle of lamplight at the kitchen table. The boys were afraid of what Pop might do if he came home and caught them using his typewriter we were so engrossed in our newspaper she forgot to be afraid of anything.

Then there was a great knocking at the kitchen door. The dog jumped up and yapped. Pop yelled, **'Open this damn door.'**

We took away the chair and Pop came in shaking himself as if he was the dog. He was drenched and had a wild look about him. 'What in the name of tarnation are you kids still doing up?' He didn't say much about the typewriter but made everybody go to bed while he sat on a bit reading. When Rinkie woke up the next morning he was beside her in the bed. She wondered if he had been cold. She climbed out over him and went to look in the kitchen. Our newspaper was still there on the table; just a few sheets of paper lying about but the typewriter was back in the other room where it belonged.

The morning dawned bright and clear, we went out to inspect the damage. It had been a hurricane. There were a few trees down and lots of limbs and branches lay about the place. There was one tree across the road further down and men came to saw it up. The telephone lines were down and the electric wires also. Other people had had to sit in lamplight too. This was the way life went on. A real line storm and a pretend line storm telescoped into one composite memory so Rinkie couldn't always tell which was which.

Chapter Twenty-eight

Keeping House

Somebody gave us pies for Thanksgiving but we had trouble cooking them; the oven wasn't hot enough. We lived mostly on eggs, cans of stuff and corn flakes and shredded wheat. Canned soup was easy; but Rinkie still didn't like tomato. Pop did cook when he was home. We still took lunches to school and made our own of what was there. Sometimes it was just 'store bought bread' with salt and pepper. We sneaked money for candy whenever we could.

We could put food 'on the bill' at Honon's Store but not candy. I don't know if that was Mr.Honon's rule or Pop's. We were used to spending time looking in the glass fronted candy display drooling. But we found a way to get candy. There was a big jar of the wartime silver 'cheap' pennies' I think they were 1943 pennies. Long before Ma died we had started pinching them; now the jar was empty. We had to rely on 'found money' or Pop might sometimes give us some. Hal had inherited the paper round so he did have money; Jimmy took it over when Hal left for the navy.

Without Ma there to see to things, the kitchen was unnaturally empty. There were never any good cooking smells. Flies fell off the too full flypapers; little spills of sugar and jelly attracted them in hoards. Even when the weather got cold the flypapers hung swinging from the ceiling blistering with dead flies. The spills grew matted and stiff on the oilcloth. We just didn't know how to keep house.

One day Rinkie thought she would clean it up and make bread. She wasn't too good at cooking but she had always made bread with Ma so she knew exactly how to do it. First she cleared a place on the end of the table and wiped it clean as she had done lots of times before. I guess she felt guilty somewhere inside because she knew she maybe should do it everyday like Ma had and keep the edges of the table clean and sweep the floor. She was in by herself and she knew Pop would be home in the afternoon because he had left early in the morning. She decided she would surprise him. The stove wasn't lit so she got kindling and wood and newspaper and made up the fire in the firebox. It was full of dead ashes but she just left them for next time and started the fire on top. It blazed up brightly as it should and the kindling 'caught'. So she put in lots of sticks as Ma used to and put the lid on. That was the fire ready.

There was still yeast in the little brown jar in the cupboard and flour in the three-quarter empty sack. She got down the big bowl, the ochre one with the white inside. The white was dusty and had the marks of many stirrings where some of the shiny stuff had worn off.

I guess I better wash it.

She took it over to the pail and splashed some water in and rinsed it out into the full sink. Now it had more marks of streaky dust rivers but she didn't mind.

Got to eat a peck of dirt before you die anyway.

She was ready. She put in the cupfuls of flour, added three teaspoonfuls of salt and some of the oleo they now used instead of butter. She mixed it together taking care to add air by lifting the handfuls of flour and letting it drop back into the bowl. She remembered Mama's far away look when she had made bread. Rinkie hadn't bothered to mix the capsule of yellow food colour into the oleo so it was white instead of yellow. She usually loved to mix in the dye to turn oleo into butter; it had been her job every since they had first used oleo when Ma didn't make butter and the war was on. But today she had to think of the bread. It was then she remembered she had to heat the milk to make the yeast work. She mixed some milk with water and so to be quick she lit the oil burner and heated it there. You could turn the oil burner up high and it would heat really fast. She put it in with the yeast and just in time remembered to add sugar. Then she had to wait for the yeast to froth.

I should'ave done it first.

It took so long she was afraid she had 'killed it' with too hot water but then at last the little bubbles appeared around the edges and it frothed up. So she got on with the mixing. That was the hardest part, stirring with the big spoon to make the sticky mess behave itself. When it was almost mixed enough she put flour over the end of the table and turned the sticky lump out just like she had seen Ma do thousands of times.

Kneading was harder on her own. But she kept at it until the sticky lump was smooth and 'elastic' just like Ma used to do. Then she wiped her hands down her sides and put the bowl on the back part of the stove to rise, just like Ma used to do. Then it was time to wait. So she went off to have a swing just like she used to do. She still loved to swing, and sing and dream stories. Now she liked to remember things like they were before. She spent lots of time remembering and inventing and telling herself stories until sometimes she couldn't tell which was which. She told everybody that Mama had died in a nice cool store and she had smiled before she died. In her head she could picture Mama's smiling face. Not like she was in the coffin but with kind eyes.

She jumped off the swing and went in to look at the rising. But the bread was still a little lump in the bottom of the bowl; it had not grown any bigger. Rinkie looked at the mess in the kitchen with flour everywhere and decided she had better clean it up before Pop came. He might be mad. It took her a long time. Still the bread wasn't risen, not one tiny little bit. So she went off to play with her dolls. Her best doll had a floppy body and stiff arms and legs. It was quite like a real baby. Then she got hungry and went back to the kitchen to get something to eat. Still the bread hadn't risen, not at all.

Pop'll be real mad if he finds out I wasted all that flour.

She grabbed the bowl and took it out to the dooryard in a panic. She was going to bury it but that would take too long so she found a hole in the stone wall fence beside the dooryard and stuffed the dough in there. It wouldn't all fit in the same one so she put little handfuls into lots of little holes. By now the morning sun felt warm on her back as she knelt down getting rid of the dough. Then she went down to the brook and washed the bowl in the running water and arrived home with it full of shiny stones.

She was sitting playing with the stones in the sunshine at the kitchen door when she noticed something funny; there were two or three chickens left and they were in the dooryard along by the fence. There they were pecking at something white. Little billows of dough were sticking out from the stones.

It must'ave been too cold in the kitchen. The sun made it rise.

She looked inside the stove and found that her fire had only burned for a little while and the sticks were all still there with only little edges of black. The fire hadn't caught and the stove was too cold. But Pop caught her because he came round the corner before she could shoo the chickens away. She thought he would be SO mad but he only laughed and laughed and told the story of the damn chickens to somebody on the telephone. He didn't tell the boys though and so she didn't get teased.

As time passed we established some sort of routine. I can't remember what it was but we must have eaten because that winter Rinkie got very fat. There was a Diner about two miles from Hawleyville; a nice lady called Mrs.Colepaugh owned it. (I don't think that is the way you spell it but Pop always called her Mrs. Hotfoot.) He had given her money to feed us whenever we went there. So we would often go to 'Hot Foot's Diner'. It was fun to sit up on the high stools and order whatever you wanted. We talked with the truck drivers and had a laugh. One night Pop came in on his way home and caught us eating hot dogs and beans. He gave Mrs. Hot Foot HELL.

They can eat that junk at home. I want you to give them real food when they come here.

He was mad in the way only Pop could get mad. So then we had to eat 'proper food' but Mrs.Colepaugh would put in a hotdog now and then. We always finished with pie and ice cream.

Chapter Twenty-nine

Fooling Around

Halsie, Jimmy and I often hitchhiked into Newtown to see the movies on a Friday night. Even if we weren't lucky enough to get a ride walking one way wasn't too bad. We mostly got a ride though. We then hung around until the end of the show. We might see the whole programme through twice. Then the cameraman, who lived in Danbury and had to drive past the end of the Hawleyville Road, would give us a lift to within a mile of our house. We walked singing and laughing down the dark road, past Bakey's farm, past the swimming hole and up home. Sometimes Hal bought Coca-Cola. He said if you drank it with aspirin you would get drunk. We often acted drunk but we weren't.

Rinkie had always played games with the boys where she was the 'nurse'. As in most big families there had been a lot of fighting, pushing, poking, teasing, tickling and other benign forms of fooling about. Usually somebody was around to stop things from going too far. Now they had to govern themselves. Rinkie didn't know about 'teenagers' and 'testosterone' and I guess nobody else thought about it. She also didn't really know what part she was supposed to play when they began a new kind of 'fooling around'. So she cooperated and just let them do what ever they wanted; they wanted to use their tool. They never did it when Pop was around and, of course, it was a new thing since Ma died.

It was sort of exciting; she liked to be included but she also knew it was somehow wrong but she didn't really know why. Rinkie was fascinated by the way in which their pecker could grow and shrink. She had a look with a mirror to see if anything was happening to her. She knew boys and girls were different and she knew why but she thought she would check anyway just in case. Hers didn't look any different except that it was growing a little red curly hair on the edges; she had always wanted curly hair. Pop mostly slept 'bare assed', if he wasn't in his long johns, so she knew about his. It looked funny, long and a bit like a rooster's waddle. She never saw it stick out like the boys.

She had noticed her chest beginning to grow. Although they didn't have regular meals Rinkie was becoming a bit fat. One day she was walking to the store wearing a white blouse that had an inset of lace on both sides of the front. The stitching had given way and one of her titties just peeped out of the hole. A neighbour stopped her and told her she mustn't wear the blouse until it was mended. Rinkie could sew a bit and when she got home she threaded up a needle and pulled the two sides together into a little bunchy row of stitching. So she could do mending! She was unaccountably ashamed of the incident. The boy's pants were still on the chair in the kitchen as they were to stay as long as Rinkie lived at home.

Rinkie felt sorry for Pop sometimes. His face looked sad. She would often wake in the night to find him in bed beside her. It happened more and more. When she felt his pecker against her back she thought she knew what was coming next. So she moved away over to the very edge of the bed as far as she could get. His hands would then stroke her back and she really liked that. Then he might begin to cry and she didn't want him to. She learned to lie very still when she woke to find him there and not let him know she was awake. Then he did whatever he was doing and she didn't have to do anything but lie still. But as far as she knew he never tried to put his pecker into her, just against her back. I think he thought she didn't know he was there.

The fact of Pop in her bed was not comforting the way sleeping with Ma had been. It erased the good feeling she used to have when she laid in bed remembering the stories and songs and what it had been like lying against Mama's solid presence. Even her dolls felt lonely because she didn't sing to them.

Somehow the winter passed. She can't remember anything about that Christmas.

Chapter Thirty
Learning the Hard Way

As the year went along, Rinkie learned lots of things that were to stay with her throughout her life. One of the first was never, ever cool a hot flat iron in a bucket of water. The flat irons had little detachable handles and they were put to heat on the kitchen stove. In an emergency they could be heated by putting them on an iron skillet on the oil burner. She knew how to test them to see if they were hot enough to use. You turned them over and spit on the plate. If the spit jumped around and sizzled, they were hot enough. What she didn't know was how to find out if they were too hot. She had made a few brown scorch marks on a few things already. Then she remembered how Ma used to put a piece of newspaper with salt on it on the end of the table to run the iron over to take off marks and how sometimes this newspaper got scorched and she would mummer, 'Too hot'. What she didn't remember was what to do about it.

This day she wanted to iron something and had heated the iron on the oil burner. When she tried it out it was way too hot so she went over to the water pail and plunged the bottom of the iron into the water. The steam came hissing up; she dropped the iron and watched three fingers of her right hand as they went red and then swelled into blisters that turned them into double the size they ought to be. Nobody was home and so she just wrapped her hand in a piece of cloth having first rubbed it with butter. She was somehow ashamed of this so she didn't tell anybody and nobody noticed for a day or two. The blisters gradually grew less painful and one day she heated up a needle in a match flame and stuck them and watched the water drain away. By then somebody had seen them and told her that was what to do. She wrapped the weeping fingers in a bandage of sorts and gradually they got better. She didn't make that mistake again. She got quite good at heating irons.

It was just nearly Christmas, Rinkie was very excited; she was going to be in a concert at school and they were going to go to Newtown Town Hall too. One year she had stood in a line with the other children and sang 'Jolly Old St. Nicholas' with actions but this time she was in a choir. They had to have a white blouse or a white shirt. She had one but it was dirty so she washed it

and because this was a special occasion she decided to starch it too. Ma used to starch things when somebody needed it specially. She found a half full package of starch and decided to make 'hot water starch' like it said on the package. But there wasn't very much water left so she only used what there was. She used all of the starch. It was a bit thick but she managed to thoroughly soak the blouse and hung it out on the line to drip. When it was almost dry she brought it in and rolled it up the way Ma used to, taking care to smooth out what creases she could.

Goodie. It's beginning to feel starched already.

The kitchen stove was alight so she was able to heat the irons there. She had three of them all ready and the ironing sheet ready on the table. Taking great care to ensure the bottoms were clean by rubbing them across the newspaper coated with salt, she ironed the blouse. First she did the back, like Ma used to do, then the collar, then the fronts and last of all the sleeves. It was really hard to get the creases out and she was forced to take the pail and fetch some water before she could

finish. She needed it to 'damp down' the places when she had 'ironed in' creases. When it was done she was quite worried because it had some streaks on it from the bottom of the iron but she decided it would 'do'. She went to lay it across the back of a chair ready for school the next day but it wouldn't fold so she put it at the bottom of her bed. In the morning she tried to put it on but the fronts were stuck to the back and the sleeves were stuck together.

She ripped it apart and forced her hands down the sleeves. Tears of frustration ran down her cheeks as she stomped her way to school wearing what felt like a cardboard box with the cuffs flapping and the buttons not done up properly.

Damnation! Judas H Priest!

At least it's white.

By the time she got to school her neck itched from where the collar stuck into it but at least her arms worked now. She still crackled a bit when she moved and she had to sit carefully at the desk so as not to mess up the smooth front.

She remembered once when she had been in a Maypole Dance at school. That was when she was little. Mama had made her a new dress to match the colour of the ribbon she was to suppose to hold. She couldn't remember the colour but she remembered the feeling. Mama had starched that dress so it ballooned out when she danced and twirled the ribbon in and out with the other children so that they ended up with a woven pattern all down the Maypole before they danced it back up the pole again. That was the only time Rinkie could remember Mama coming to school with the other mothers to sit on a long bench outside. She had walked all the way there and home with Rinkie at the end. She had lemonade and cookies and Mrs. Clarke sat beside her.

Rinkie tried to remember everything she could. She could really remember very far back. Like when she was just very, very small and they were having a baby shower for Rainey. It was at Rainey's father's house; her mother was dead. Rinkie had never been to a shower before. It was at night and they didn't have lamps with wicks and chimneys so the house glowed with lights shining through coloured shades. Mama was there; Rinkie had a special job. There was a baby carriage piled high with presents wrapped in beautiful coloured paper and tied with ribbons. It was her job to push this surprise into where Rainey was sitting. Everybody clapped; she thought they must have been clapping for her because she looked so nice in her new dress and specially whitened shoes. They had sandwiches and jello.

Rinkie loved babies, still. Her dolls were her best friends now even though she had turned ten. She felt sorry for them because they didn't have new clothes much now when Ma wasn't there to help her. She looked through the Montgomery Ward catalogue and found a beautiful flannelette baby blanket for forty-three cents. It came in blue, yellow, white and pink. She decided on the pink. It took her a long time to write out the order. She found the forty-three cents and taped it to a piece of cardboard like she had seen Ma do. You had to send postage stamps so she had to wait until she got to the store to get them and add them to the order. Then she addressed the envelope and stuck on the stamp. After that she called in everyday at the store, which was also the post-office to see if there was anything in Box 25. There were often things there but nothing for her. She sort of gave up hope. Then one day Pop came in with a small package and tossed it to her.

I don't know what this is, what have you been buying from the catalogue?

Nothin… it's for my doll.

You're too big for dolls.

Maybe she was but the flannelette blanket was lovely, so soft and warm and cosy. She wrapped it round her doll and cradled and sang to her.

There now. Don't cry.
Mama's got you.
Rock-a by baby
In the treetops.

Her doll was quite a big one and Rinkie sometimes put it beside her when she thought Pop might visit in the night.

When it was nearly Easter, Rinkie began to worry about having a new dress for Sunday School.

'Mama; Mama'

The cry volleyed around the too empty room and hung suspended, like a dead fly stuck to flypaper hung in the kitchen where her mother used to sit.

'Mama', whispered an echo she almost didn't recognize as her own.

Easter was coming and *everybody* had to have a new Easter outfit. She told Pop. 'I've gotta have something new to wear to Sunday School' Mama had *always* made her a new dress for Easter out of one of the many feedbags all washed and folded with their patterns and colours matched into pairs of threes or even fours. There was plenty of stuff but she could only sew patchwork and doll's clothes.

Pop looked at her with haunted eyes, ' We'll go to JC Penny's'

The car journey to Danbury to buy 'store bought' clothes was strangely unfamiliar with just Pop and her riding together in the front seat.

In Penny's she had smelled the new dresses hanging in rows; their pastel colours gathered and puffed into a colouring box of choosing. She went down the row touching each in turn. At every suggestion or tentative 'try up' to herself, Pop had frowned a 'no' at her.

At length they came across rows of grey skirts which were 'marked down'. She was hustled into a curtained room to try on skirt after skirt. She had gotten very fat during the winter since Ma died. The skirts that went around her and zipped together came down to her ankles. The one finally settled upon was so long it dusted the tops of her white canvas shoes. 'A gray skirt is best', said Pop' 'it'll do a long time.' As a concession to spring she had been allowed to choose a sweater in pastel yellow. It was 1945. She was eleven and a half.

She remembered taking the skirt to Pat, the one sister who lived nearby. Pop had conceded that it was 'too long'. She was to ask to get it shortened but not to cut off any of the material. Her sister had said, 'No. It's fine as it is'. It wasn't. She had worn it anyway on Easter Sunday and nearly everyday to school right up until summer. The yellow sweater gradually took on the grey of the skirt as it attracted unwashed grime.

Rinkie finished off her last year at Land's End School. She would be in the Seventh grade next year and the bigger kids were bussed to Newtown.

Things were changing everywhere.

There was the war. It existed mainly in the crackling of the battery radio which gave out reports from foreign correspondents from places too remote to be imagined with strange names and fronts and lines: the Russian front, the Maginot line. And she never really sorted out the Axis and Allies. We hadn't had a radio before so it was also our first experience of 'The Lone Ranger' and 'The Grand Ol' Oprey' and songs like 'Don't sit under the apple tree with anyone else but me, anyone else but me, anyone else but me'. We had always had a phonograph but the records were all old ones.

Hawleyville had a unique warning system of air raids. It stood in the top corner of the triangle of ground upon which the school sat. It was a large wooden construction made from railroad ties and on it hung an iron train wheel with a chunk taken out. Leaning against the post beside it was a sledgehammer too heavy for us elementary kids to lift. If there was an air raid, my Carl who worked at Land's End Farm, or anybody else handy had to hit the warning of impending attack upon this gong. The planes never came but we practised anyway.

It was always with the greatest fear that Rinkie crouched with the others under her school desk until the fire siren told us the 'attack' was over or not coming that day. Hawleyville had a volunteer fire brigade and at first the fire siren sounded to signal an air raid but the volunteers got tired of scrambling for nothing. Therefore the 'Railroad train wheel in Hawleyville' became a local claim to fame. Pop made such fun of it that I now suspect it was his idea in the first place.

By the end of the wartime draft, we had a flag with four stars hanging in our window - one for Johnnie, Benny, Jiggy and Billy - all in the Navy. Carl had a protected occupation as he was a farmer and George worked in a munitions factory. Hal and Jimmy joined the Navy as soon as they could but the war was over by then. Rinkie started school in 1939 a couple of years before American joined the Allies.

We knew all about the war efforts and Jimmy, Hal and I spent much time doing our bit. We had cap pistols but no caps so we spent hours cutting newspaper into strips and rolling it up to feed into the guns. It didn't make the right noise but it was better than nothing and we had to be prepared. We dug trenches and bunkers to hide in if an air raid happened when we weren't at school and didn't have a desk to hide under. Every time an airplane flew over I crouched down sure that this was it; we were gonna get it this time.

But we didn't.

At school we learned about the poor children of Britain who needed help and had no toys and food. We were urged to bring in a shoebox full of essentials like soap, toothbrushes, candy bars and socks and toys. Rinkie had begged Mama for these things we 'had to have' for the poor children in Britain suffering in the war with their houses bombed. She was so proud of her collection of things and did not think it in the least odd that she didn't have a toothbrush or toothpowder in a tin nor a new wash cloth with a sewed edge like we sent them, nor new white socks. We did have Tootsie Rolls sometimes, and 'Guess What's' - candy wrapped in a paper cylinder with a joke and a small toy or puzzle.

The war nearly ended in the spring after Ma died. Pop answered the telephone one afternoon. He was working nights at that time and slept in the day. He jumped out of bed grabbing a newspaper from the floor as he did so to cover his pecker; he always slept with nothing on. He started shouting and jumping up and down waving his arms and the newspaper. ' It's over. VE Day today. They've got the sons of bitches. Jesus H Christ. They've got the God Dammed Sons of Bitches. Heil Hitler my ass.'

Looking exactly like a turkey's waddle, his pecker waggled up and down as he danced and jumped about. That was VE day. Before the real end of the war – VJ Day – Rinkie's world had changed dramatically.

Chapter Thirty-one
Leaving Hawleyville

That last year at home didn't last quite a year. During it Hal went into the navy so Jimmy and Rink were the only kids at home. Pop still worked shifts on the railroad. Jimmy had his paper round and Rinkie sometimes went with him part of the way especially if they were going to 'HotFoot's' for supper. Jimmy went on the bus to Sandy Hook to school; he dropped from being a straight 'A' student to failing in most areas. Rinkie loved school and worked very hard but she still couldn't spell. There were lots and lots of books in the house. Pop loved books; so did Rinkie. She devoured books. It didn't matter to her that she couldn't pronounce all of the words she read for the sense of the story and drama.

There were some books Pop had put into brown paper covers and she wasn't supposed to have them but she did anyway. Afterwards she was never sure if he did that to ensure they read them or because he didn't want them messed up. Either way, Rinkie attempted almost anything. She read her way through all of the children's books reading things like 'The Wizard of Oz', 'Gulliver's Travels', and stories of

Greek and Roman history then on to Milton, Keats, Walt Witman, and Ralph Waldo Emmerson. She really liked 'The Scarlet Letter',Silas Marner' and 'The Grapes of Wrath'. She cried over the poor people with no food and for 'Epie in the 'tole hole' and saw her golden hair and poor Silas who had to tie her up to keep her safe when he did his weaving. She dreamed and made up stories of her own endlessly.

There were things she was supposed to do and she didn't always. One Sunday she got ready to go to Sunday school as she usually did. It was a lovely sunny day and she whitened her shoes and wore the grey skirt and yellow sweater. She had an apple to eat on the bus. Pop was just coming down from the backhouse when she asked him to braid her hair and give her money for the collection.

You can't go. There's too much to do here. You haven't washed the dishes for two days.

Rinkie threw down the apple with such force that it smashed against the 'sitting rock' beside the house. She screamed and swore and stamped her feet but he wouldn't give her money for the collection and she couldn't go without it. She sobbed her way through the dishes and cleaning up the kitchen not caring that she got very wet with the splashing when she emptied the water in the dooryard. Pop hid behind the newspaper. When it was much too late he finally offered to do her hair but she wouldn't let him.

He went out for a walk in the woods. He was gone a long time. Maybe that was when he decided.

Rinkie was never quite sure how things were decided. Nobody talked to her about it. But, once school was finished in June, she somehow got to Tonie's at the farm about ten miles away in Redding. She can't remember who took her or how it was planned. It was a whole new wonderful life. The house was old and falling down in places. It had electricity but no water inside. The water was carried up from the creamery. It was a small dairy farm that produced, bottled and delivered un-pasteurised milk.

Tonie now had two babies. Georgie was nearly two and Bucky, the baby who had come to Ma's funeral inside Tonie's tummy, could sit up by himself on a blanket under the big trees. Rinkie spent most of the summer playing with them. She had left her dolls in Hawleyville but she didn't miss them. They were like dolls come alive. They had dungarees and matching shirts in the most wonderful colours. She didn't mind changing smelly diapers even.

She learned lots of things that summer. She learned not to be afraid of thunder and lightning in case the kids caught her fear; Tonie didn't want them crying for every little thundershower that rumbled. She found out all about cows. One job was to go and fetch them from the field across the road when milking time came. She hung about the barn and watched the milking, always willing to put the washing cloth in the bucket of water or carry a milk pail up to be emptied into the strainer on the churn. There was a farm boy there for the summer. He was not too much older than she was and she watched him carefully. Sam, Tonie's husband was big and smiley and gave her hugs; nobody else ever gave her hugs.

Sam took her on tractor rides, let her ride up on the hay truck as they pitched the hay into a pile and took it back to the barn. Her job was to pack it down. Sam often joined her on the top of the truck in the hay when his brother drove, to build the load so it wouldn't topple. On the drive back to the barn from the fields they would lie and look up as the sky went by overhead and they were tumbled to and fro. It was friendly smelling the new hay and getting a bumpy ride. He had lots to do because he went everyday to deliver the milk as well as doing one milking. It was a family business. There were three brothers, two farms and 'the old man', their father.

Towards the end of the summer Tonie told her she was going to go back to Hawleyville to pack up her things to go and live with Aunt Maude. Sam took her on the milk round the next day. He left her in Hawleyville and said he would be back for her in a few days.

Rinkie knew who Aunt Maude was. She was Ma's sister and she lived not far away in Bethel. Rinkie had never visited her nor could she remember exactly who she was but she knew she had been at the funeral. She just couldn't think what she looked like.

It was quiet and dusty and strange in the hot empty house as she waited on the day Sam was to come for her. The flies buzzed in the kitchen. She had her

cardboard box of things ready. Somebody, Pop maybe, had already put some of her clothes in and she added to it the other things she wanted. She couldn't take the books because they were Pop's. She didn't have many clothes that fit. Tonie had bought her two new dresses at the beginning of the summer. She had torn one when she had caught it on the side as she jumped out of the back of Sam's pickup truck about the first or second time she wore it but Tonie had mended it into a kind of jumper suit with shorts at the bottom to hide the tear. It was clean so she decided to wear that. Pop had gone off to work and she waited with Skippy, the dog for Sam to come. She doesn't remember where Jimmy was.

Rinkie was sitting with her doll wrapped in the pink flannelette blanket when the dog started barking and Sam came in from the driveway. He picked up her box, stuffed the doll on top and loaded her and her box into the front of the pickup truck. Then they went off on the rest of the milk round until he came to Aunt Maude's house in Bethel.

It was a wooden house on a little hill in a street with other houses. Aunt Maude lived upstairs; her steps were on the outside. Sam carried in the box with the doll's legs sticking out of the top. Rinkie went up and Aunt Maude opened the screen door. They went in to a small very clean house. She took them into the kitchen and Sam put down the milk; he was not her usual milkman but he brought milk this day. Rinkie stood up against the refrigerator making herself as small as possible. Sam didn't stay long and as he was going Aunt Maude turned to Rinkie. She called her 'Vera' and said, 'I've only taken you because it is my duty to do so'.

That was the end of Rinkie's childhood. She was not quite twelve.

July 4th 1945

Acknowledgements

My thanks must go to all my family and friends, who have cheered me on to record images and stories of my 'Hawleyville Days' and 'Wild Strawberry Times' before they too disappear like the terrain of my childhood. Especial thanks is due to Iain who showed great patience in helping me to conquer the necessary technology and who never doubted I should persist in getting it into print. Also to Joe and Ben who have always shown how much they love their 'Baba'and who liked to hear about 'when you were little', especially the naughty bits.

The information about Hawleyville in its heyday was taken from:

Newtown Trails Book, fifth edition, by Mary Mitchell and Albert Goodrich, The Friends of the C H Booth Library, Newtown Ct, 2000

My sister Tonie's (C R Williams) memoirs can be seen at the C H Booth Library in "Newtown Remembered: More Stories of the 20th Century."2005 Ed. Andrea Zimmermann et al also lodged in the C H Booth Library.

My thanks also to Andrea Zimmermann at the C H Booth Library Newtown who has been most helpful in answering my queries and giving supportive advice.

The page from the Sears Roebuck Catalogue was downloaded from the internet.